The South Carolina State House Grounds

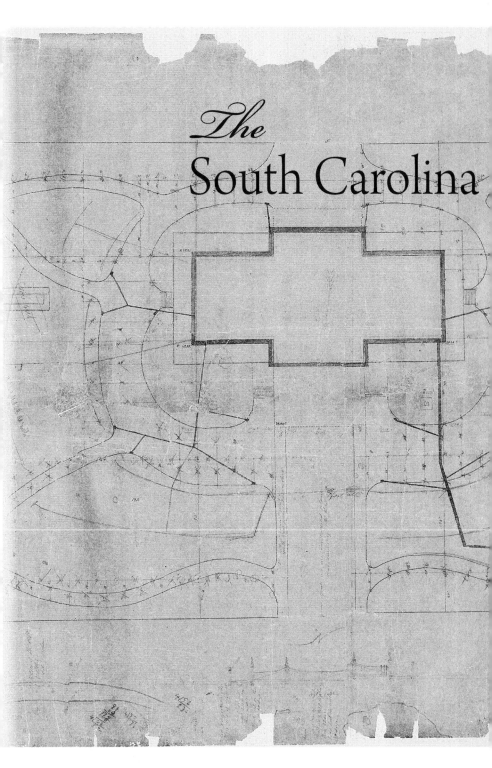

The
South Carolina

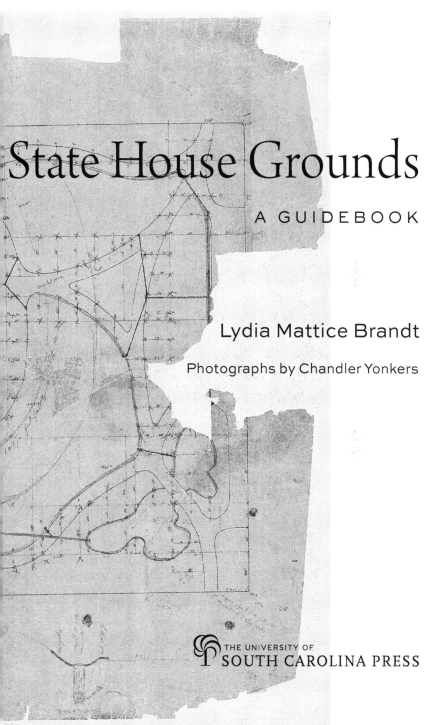

State House Grounds

A GUIDEBOOK

Lydia Mattice Brandt

Photographs by Chandler Yonkers

THE UNIVERSITY OF
SOUTH CAROLINA PRESS

Published by the University of South Carolina Press
Columbia, South Carolina 29208

www.uscpress.com

Manufactured in the United States of America

30 29 28 27 26 25 24 23 22 21
10 9 8 7 6 5 4 3 2 1

Library of Congress Cataloging-in-Publication Data
can be found at http://catalog.loc.gov/.

ISBN: 978–1-64336–178–9 (paperback)
ISBN: 978–1-64336–179–6 (ebook)

Publication of this book was made possible in part
by the generous support of Historic Columbia and
the Richland County Conservation Commission.

Contents

Acknowledgments   vii
A Brief Timeline of South Carolina History   ix
Abbreviations   xiii
Map of the State House Grounds   xiv

Introduction: Defining the State House Grounds   1

One. Building and Challenging a
Sovereign State House (1790–1877)   7

South Carolina State House   9
Swanson Lunsford Grave   17
George Washington Monument   19
Sculpture on the North Façade of the State House   24
Palmetto Monument   29

Two. Jim Crow and the
State House Beautiful (1877–1968)   34

Plans for the State House Landscape   36
South Carolina Monument to the Confederate Dead
(Confederate Monument)   43
Wade Hampton Monument   46
Partisan Generals Monument   51
Monument to the Women of the Confederacy
(Confederate Women's Monument)   54
Spanish-American War Monuments   58
James Marion Sims Monument   64
Jefferson Davis and Robert E. Lee
Memorial Highway Markers   67

Memorial Trees on the State House Grounds   71
John C. Calhoun State Office Building   74
Wade Hampton State Office Building   77
Stars on the State House and Marker
for the First State House   78
Benjamin Ryan Tillman Monument   82
Liberty Bell Replica   86
Confederate Battle Flag   87

Three. Building for Bureaucracy
(1969–Present)   90

James Francis Byrnes Monument   93
Redesign of the State House Grounds   96
Capitol Complex Master Plan   99
Furman McEachern Jr. Parking Garage   104
Edgar A. Brown Building and
Solomon Blatt Building   106
L. Marion Gressette Building   108
Rembert C. Dennis Building   110
Richardson Square Marker   113
Capitol Complex Marker   114
Columbia Bicentennial Time Capsule   115
Strom Thurmond Monument   117
African American History Monument   120
South Carolina Law Enforcement Memorial and
South Carolina Armed Forces Monument   125

Appendix: Maps of the South Carolina
State House Grounds, 1790–present   131
Abbreviations Used in Notes   137
Notes   139
Index   171

Acknowledgments

This book is a testament to the strong network of historic preservationists, architecture enthusiasts, and local historians in South Carolina. After years of researching here and there to answer questions about particular buildings or monuments, I finally resolved to write a guidebook thanks to a partnership with Historic Columbia. I am thankful to Katharine Allen, John Sherrer, Robin Waites, Chandler Yonkers, and the rest of the Historic Columbia staff for supporting it with research assistance, robust public programming, a website, and a podcast. A historic preservation grant from the Richland County Conservation Commission funded the research, guided by Nancy Stone-Collum. Margaret Dunlap and the Walker Local History Room at the Richland County Public Library provided many of the terrific historic images that helped me to understand the site's development. I am grateful to Olivia Miller for her research and organization of the book's images. Albert Hester and Chuck Lesser helped me to navigate the site physically and archivally. Lee Ann Kournegay, Fred Delk, and Richard Burts were thoughtful co-conspirators as always. Robert Weyeneth and Thomas Brown, my dear colleagues at the University of South Carolina (UofSC), offered fellowship, constructive criticism, and sounding boards for the book's issues—large and small. Mary Fesak dug in the archives at the University of Delaware when I could not. Former students Ari Robbins, Casey Lee, and Stephanie Gray conducted the excellent seed research for the Capitol Complex of the 1970s. UofSC's College of Arts and Science's Book Manuscript Finalization Support Initiative helped send the book over the finish line. It was an absolute pleasure to work with my friend and editor Ehren Foley at UofSC Press on this book, which is far better for his involvement—as well as that of the two anonymous peer reviewers who commented on the manuscript and proposal.

This book also benefited from a motley crew of architectural historians, friends, and colleagues across the South and beyond. At conferences and on bar stools and site visits, their friendship and thoughtful conversation buoyed and inspired me. I am especially thankful to Christian Anderson, Jennifer Baughn, Catherine Bishir, Katherine Chaddock, Philip Mills Herrington, Margaret Grubiak, Elizabeth Milnarik, Ben Ross, Rachel Stephens, Dell Upton, and my friends at the Vernacular Architecture Forum and the Southeast Chapter of the Society of Architectural Historians. My family was as patient with this project as they have been with every other. I thank my husband, Jake Erwin, for always stopping to read the plaque with me.

I am most grateful to the students, citizens, and friends who asked the tough questions that convinced me of the need for this book.

A Brief Timeline of
South Carolina History
(as Pertains to the State House Grounds)

1775–82

South Carolinians fight the American Revolution, with patriot militias led by Francis Marion, Andrew Pickens, Thomas Sumter, and others.

1788

South Carolina ratifies the US Constitution to join the United States.

1790

The state legislature first meets in Columbia.

1832–33

South Carolina senator John C. Calhoun leads the confrontation between the federal and state governments in the Nullification Crisis, a sectional disagreement over the constitutional right of the federal government to impose tariffs on the states that lays the groundwork for secession.

1847–48

The state's Palmetto Regiment fights for US territory in the Mexican-American War.

December 20, 1860

Confederate forces at Fort Sumter in Charleston, South Carolina, fire the first shots of the Civil War.

The South Carolina legislature votes to secede from the Union, making it the first state to join the Confederacy.

January 1, 1863
President Abraham Lincoln reads the Emancipation Proclamation, freeing enslaved African Americans in South Carolina.

February 1865
During the night of February 17–18, 1865, much of Columbia's main commercial district, more than 450 buildings in all, is destroyed during a massive fire. The flames are aided by a combination of burning cotton bales left behind by Confederate forces, high winds, and Union Army soldiers occuping the city.

April 9, 1865
Confederate general Robert E. Lee surrenders at Appomattox, Virginia, marking an end of the main military operations of the Civil War.

1865–77
The years immediately following the Confederacy's surrender, referred to as Reconstruction, in which the federal government controls the South's readmittance to the Union and Republican politicians win a majority of political offices in the state government in South Carolina.

1868
A constitutional convention meets in Charleston and adopts a new state constitution that extends voting rights to all male citizens, regardless of race.

South Carolina becomes the first and only state to elect and seat a majority–African American state legislature.

1876–77
Former Confederate general Wade Hampton III is declared the winner of a contested election as governor (serves 1877–79), ending Reconstruction and returning power to a White Democratic majority.

1890–94
Benjamin Tillman is governor of South Carolina.

1895

The state legislature passes a new constitution that disenfranchises African American voters.

1896

The US Supreme Court decides *Plessy v. Ferguson,* sanctioning "separate but equal" policy and Jim Crow laws in the South.

1898

South Carolina sends soldiers to Cuba to fight the Spanish-American War.

1933–39

President Franklin Delano Roosevelt's New Deal programs provide employment relief and funding for new construction across the state and nation during the Great Depression that followed the stock market crash of 1929.

November 10, 1939

The South Carolina Conference of the National Association for the Advancement of Colored People (NAACP) forms to advocate for Black South Carolinians and protest Jim Crow (the state's first branches chartered in Charleston and Columbia in 1917).

1941–45

America fights in World War II, bringing population growth and a boost to South Carolina's economy.

1951–55

James F. Byrnes is governor of South Carolina.

1954

The US Supreme Court declares the doctrine of "separate but equal" unconstitutional in its *Brown v. Board of Education* decision, making racial segregation illegal in public schools.

1957

South Carolina senator Strom Thurmond filibusters the Civil Rights Act of 1957, which passes to help protect African Americans' right to vote and serve on juries.

March 2, 1961

More than 200 individuals, many of them African American students from nearby Allen University and Benedict College, march on the State House grounds to protest racial segregation. The subsequent arrest of 187 protestors leads to the US Supreme Court decision *Edwards v. South Carolina* (1963), which affirms the constitutional right of citizens to petition government for redress.

1965–71

State government grows during the administration of Governor Robert Evander McNair.

January 29, 1968

South Carolina state police open fire on a segregation protest at South Carolina State College in Orangeburg.

1970–1

James Felder, I. S. Leevy Johnson, and Herbert Fielding are the first African American representatives elected to the state legislature since the late nineteenth century.

June 17, 2015

A White supremacist murders nine African Americans at Emanuel African Methodist Episcopal Church in Charleston.

Abbreviations

DAR	Daughters of the American Revolution
LBC&W	Lyles, Bissett, Carlisle & Wolff
NAACP	South Carolina Conference of the National Association for the Advancement of Colored People
SCMA	South Carolina Memorial Association
UCV	United Confederate Veterans
UDC	United Daughters of the Confederacy
UofSC	University of South Carolina, Columbia
WS&A	Wilbur Smith & Associates

The South Carolina State House Grounds

MAP KEY

Buildings:
A State House
B Trinity Cathedral
C John C. Calhoun State Office Building
D Wade Hampton State Office Building
E Rembert C. Dennis Building
F Edgar A. Brown Building
G Solomon Blatt Building
H L. Marion Gressette Building
I Furman McEachern Jr. Parking Garage

Monuments:
1 Swanson Lunsford Grave
2 Palmetto Monument
3 George Washington Monument
4 Henry Kirke Brown sculptures
5 Confederate Monument
6 Wade Hampton Monument
7 Partisan Generals Monument
8 Confederate Women's Monument
9 Sims Monument
10 Jefferson Davis Memorial Highway Marker
11 Robert E. Lee Memorial Highway Marker
12 George Washington Elms/Tribute Grove
13 Stars on State House
14 Old State House Marker
15 Benjamin Ryan Tillman Monument
16 Spanish-American War Veterans Monument
17 Mount for Spanish Cannon
18 Gun from USS *Maine*
19 Liberty Bell Replica
20 James Francis Byrnes Monument
21 Richardson Square Marker
22 Capitol Complex Marker
23 Columbia Bicentennial Time Capsule
24 Strom Thurmond Monument
25 African American History Monument
26 South Carolina Law Enforcement Memorial
27 South Carolina Armed Forces Monument

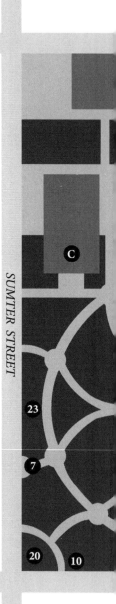

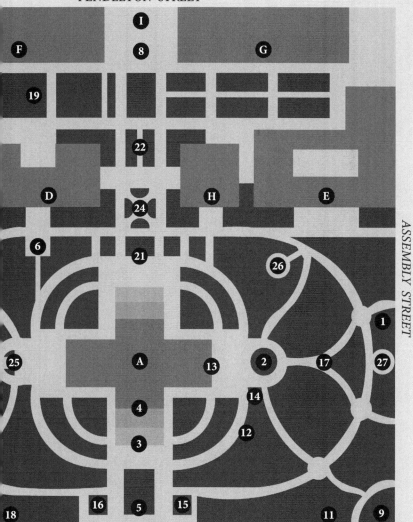

N

MAIN

PENDLETON STREET

I

8

F

G

19

22

D

24

H

E

6

21

26

1

25

A

13

2

17

27

14

4

12

3

18

16

5

15

11

9

GERVAIS STREET

MAIN

ASSEMBLY STREET

The relocation of the Wade Hampton Monument to its current location in 1969. Many of the monuments on the State House grounds have moved at least once. Courtesy of Richland Library, Columbia, S.C.

Introduction

Defining the State House Grounds

In October 1969 contractor Jimmy Orange wrapped cables under the body of a 6,600-pound statue of a horse carrying Confederate general and South Carolina governor Wade Hampton III. A crane lifted the figures off their fifteen-foot-tall base while workers poured three truckloads of concrete to support the statue at a new location elsewhere on the capitol grounds. "This is not the biggest job we've handled," Orange said, "but it's certainly one of the most interesting."[1]

The Hampton statue was one of many monuments relocated in the redesign and expansion of the State House grounds in the 1970s. The statues were rearranged to decorate the grounds and turned to face the capitol. It was logical to place Hampton's bronze figure in front of the state office building already named for him. Along with laying out new concrete walks and planting grass, moving the statue was just another task on the contractor's job list.

Monuments encapsulate complex historic events and human lives in single, seemingly unchanging figures raised on high pedestals. They freeze time while asserting an authority that also feels final and permanent. But as this unremarkable account of the Hampton Monument demonstrates, they are also physical objects that can be moved for mundane reasons.

More importantly, the meaning of monuments—or at least our perception of what they mean—can also change. When it was unveiled to thousands in November 1906 (a far cry from the "handful of spectators" who turned out to see it moved in 1969), the Hampton Monument celebrated not just a Civil War hero but also a man who

1

South Carolinians protest the murder of George Floyd at
the State House, May 30, 2020. Photograph by Crush Rush.

had led White southerners out of Reconstruction and its political
empowerment of African American men. One of the women who
fundraised for the statue passionately promoted the importance
of Hampton's postwar politics: "he saved a legion of his fellow-
country men and country women from the iron heel of oppression
and from a reign of political tyranny, ignorance, vice and degrada-
tion."[2] Following protests of the murders of African Americans by
police in the summer of 2020, calls have grown louder to eradicate
the statue of Hampton and others on the State House grounds. Advocates recognize them as symbols of the racism that underpins
America's political, economic, and social systems. While one group
saw justice in the construction of the monument, another now seeks
justice in its removal.

The South Carolina State House grounds are a work in progress. South Carolinians have constructed, altered, neglected, and
reconsidered the twenty-two-acre site for more than 230 years. And

they're still at it. This book tells the story of the literal and figural heart of the Palmetto State. It chronicles the events that occurred in and around its buildings, the stories of the people memorialized in its monuments, and the histories of the landscape itself. By recounting the intentions behind each, this guidebook considers how South Carolinians have used this place to make claims for power and identity. It argues that generations have consciously shaped this highly charged, visible, and public place to assert authority over both past and present. As South Carolina's heart and brain, the State House grounds hold tremendous power—and that power is rarely static.

What Are the State House Grounds?

People and their decisions have shaped the State House grounds over the last two centuries. They determined the architectural style of buildings, the subjects and poses of statues, the placement of monuments, the types of trees, the layouts of paths, and the sites of parking lots. South Carolinians carefully deliberated some of these features, while others were the result of neglect or default. As a whole, the State House grounds are a "cultural landscape": a series of human-built and natural components connected physically, conceptually, and aesthetically to each other over the course of hundreds of years. These relationships between buildings, monuments, paths, and natural features are physical as well as ideological. The locations or appearance of these elements matter as much as why people chose to put them in certain places, to make them look certain ways, or to juxtapose them against each other.[3] The intentions behind such decisions signify more here than many other places because the State House grounds are a public space in which momentous decisions are made for and by South Carolinians.

How Are the State House Grounds Used?

The State House grounds are the nerve center for the everyday business of the state's government. Elected legislators deliberate and determine the state's legal, financial, and social priorities in the chambers of the State House. Employees conduct the business of the state's bureaucracy and courts in the site's six office buildings.

Citizens rally for their causes by protesting and celebrating on its steps and lawns.

But the grounds are also the repository of the state's memory and values. Some South Carolinians have used the grounds to express what they believe to be important about the past and to connect those ideas to the present day. They constructed monuments, buildings, and the connective tissue between them to highlight specific events, people, or concepts in the past in order to legitimize their contemporary beliefs and actions. They have chosen to remember some things while forgetting others.

The conflict between the site's practical requirements and ideological goals has continually raised questions about what the grounds mean, how much they should cost, and who they represent. South Carolinians and their elected representatives often have taken advantage of the grounds' potential to be highly meaningful, investing money and symbolism in buildings intended to impress and monuments expected to inspire or intimidate. But at other times, they have dismissed such pomp and circumstance as a waste of taxpayers' dollars, allowing grass to die and bronze to tarnish. Although their granite and concrete appear permanent, the messages and even the physical components of the grounds have been remarkably fluid over the past two hundred years.

Who Owns the State House Grounds?

As public property, the State House grounds should represent and welcome everyone in South Carolina. The State House's broad steps can be a setting for wedding portraits or an evening workout while its grounds can be a quiet place to walk or picnic. They offer a stage for public life.

But it is not neutral space. As people jostled for political and cultural power over the past two centuries, the winners used the grounds to assert their authority and to justify their oppression of the disenfranchised. They built monuments, moved others, and made changes to the State House grounds. Their alterations were not unbiased. The landscape played an active role in asserting or contesting power and broadcasting political positions on the state's most visible platform.

With half of its monuments and buildings conceived when White South Carolinians exclusively held political power, White supremacy remains the most pervasive and persistent narrative on the grounds. Between the 1870s and 1960s, politicians and private citizens used monuments and buildings to promote racism or to celebrate their suppression of African Americans. They gave physical form and legitimacy to Jim Crow legislation that prevented Black South Carolinians from voting, accessing equal education, or participating fully in the economy.

But as society changed—often after violence and strife—so too did the State House grounds. African Americans protested on the capitol's steps and elected Black representatives to its chambers by the 1970s, reclaiming a position in determining the state's future and the appearance and meaning of the grounds. Recent additions to the site offer a more inclusive perspective but always remain in tension with other, more exclusionary narratives.

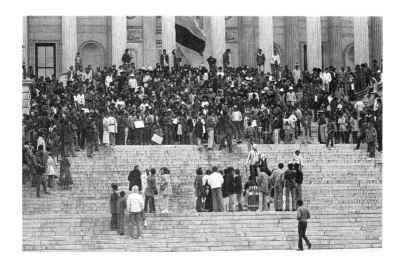

A rally for Blacks United for Action on the north steps of the State House, April 8, 1972. Courtesy of Richland Library, Columbia, S.C.

Each generation must decide what the grounds should look like as well as what they mean. Continual shifts in politics, culture, and power have resulted in a fractured and perpetually unfinished space. The grounds could never possibly represent the collective memories of every South Carolina community, nor will they ever be "finished." Its meanings cannot be fixed, nor do they have to be mutually exclusive. A single person can be proud of the grounds and at the same time feel frustrated—or even disgusted—by some of the ideas celebrated there.

How Might You Use This Book?

History and memory are different things. While humans research and write history, choosing one source over another to make specific arguments, they construct memory much more collectively, organically, and emotionally. The South Carolina State House grounds tell a distinct history of the state's *memory*. The monuments, buildings, and relationships between them reveal stories of what people wanted to remember at certain times and for certain reasons, not objective narratives. The grounds are significant for what they can tell us about how South Carolinians have seen the past through the lens of the present.

The entries that follow tell the individual histories of each monument, building, or group of buildings on the South Carolina State House grounds. They are arranged chronologically by order of their completion and emphasize the processes of designing, erecting, and using the works over the histories that might be represented or recalled.[4] Thus, to learn more about Wade Hampton, check out a biography mentioned in the guidebook's endnotes. To understand why White South Carolinians wanted to memorialize him on the State House grounds in 1906 or move his monument in 1969, read on.

ONE

Building and Challenging
a Sovereign State House
(1790–1877)

The rich plantation owners elected to lead South Carolina after the formation of the United States did not initially invest in a grand government building for their fledgling state capital. The first State House in Columbia, built in 1786–90, remained inadequate and the grounds unfinished for the first half of the nineteenth century. While leading national debates over state sovereignty in the 1830s–40s, the state's politicians finally agreed that a new, impressive state capitol could serve the legislature's administrative needs and convey South Carolina's economic and political strength. Construction began on the current State House in the 1850s with a copy of a speech by Senator John C. Calhoun, the patron saint of secession, placed in the cornerstone and plans for a sculptural program celebrating slavery for its new façade. The new building's granite walls were far from completion when the first shots of the Civil War were fired at Fort Sumter just off the state's coastline in 1861. Federal troops burned the eighteenth-century State House and damaged the walls of the new capitol in February 1865, just two months before the end of the war.

The Confederacy's defeat and the dawn of Reconstruction only reinforced the tattered, unfinished State House as contested territory. Emphasizing the reversal of the building's initial proslavery symbolism, the first government to occupy the structure was the only majority-Black state legislature in the history of the United States. Over its almost decade in power and amid constant racial violence, this biracial Republican body enacted legislation that empowered African Americans, ensured universal male suffrage, and cracked down on the Ku Klux Klan, all within the walls of this former monument to slavery.

This first phase of the State House grounds' history established the tensions that would forever define the site. On the one hand, those in power used it as a trophy to celebrate their victories and to vanquish their enemies. On the other, fiscal hawks were wary of spending money to embellish it. Politicians danced between making very expensive, deliberate changes to the grounds and allowing neglect or haphazard, cheap alterations. Private citizens saw opportunities to improve the grounds when public bodies refused. Few saw the site as a coherent whole.

South Carolina State House

First State House in Columbia, built 1786–ca. 1790; burned 1865

Current State House, built 1856–1903
John Rudolph Niernsee, Frank McHenry Niernsee,
Frank Milburn, et al., architects

South Carolina built two State Houses in Columbia's city center after joining the Union in 1788.[1] The first was constructed soon after the capital was moved from Charleston in 1786. The current capitol was begun in the 1850s and not finished until 1903. Its high site, rigid symmetry, and cross-shaped plan complement and center the city's grand orthogonal grid. Impressive stairs lead to Classical Revival porticos on the north and south elevations, creating matching façades that reach out to the twenty-two acres of landscaped grounds. The dome, one of the last features of the building to be completed, sits atop an exuberant cast-iron lobby while the wings to east and west house the Senate and House chambers, respectively. Interruptions, ineptitude, and the legislature's alternating refusal and inability to commit funding to the State House ensured that it remained under construction for more than half a century.

When the General Assembly convened in its first Columbia State House in January 1790, the building was unfinished. Facing Main Street (where the west wing of the State House sits now), this two-story frame structure was among the earliest purpose-built state capitols constructed after the American Revolution. Although far more modest, its temple-front portico was in keeping with the neoclassical style of Thomas Jefferson's Virginia State Capitol (built 1785–88) and Charles Bulfinch's Massachusetts State House (built 1795–98).[2]

Calls for improvements, more office space, and a fireproof addition began almost immediately.[3] In 1805 a visitor described the

The first State House in Columbia, first occupied by the
legislature in 1790. Courtesy of South Caroliniana Library,
University of South Carolina, Columbia, S.C.

still-incomplete structure as "entirely void of anything like just
proportion" with doors that were "never shut," apparently allowing goats to come in and out.[4] Regardless of whether it was actually
overrun with farm animals, the wooden building was cramped and
susceptible to fire, threatening the safety of the government records
stored there. Despite numerous attempts over the following decades
to appropriate funds to repair the capitol or to build a new fireproof
addition, the legislature repeatedly failed to act.[5]

Desire to build a monument to South Carolina's most revered
political figure, Senator John C. Calhoun, buoyed the practical
needs for a fireproof building following his death in 1850. The ve-
hemently proslavery and secessionist governor Whitemarsh Benjamin Seabrook called for the purchase a block to the east, across
Main Street from the State House, for a "monument to receive his

remains, composed entirely of the products of our soil, be erected in the centre; and that the grounds, skillfully ornamented with shrubbery, be converted into a public walk."[6] The legislature commissioned Charleston-based architect Peter Hjalmar Hammarskold to build a granite structure for offices and record storage with hopes that it could also be the first section of a larger building that would soon replace the State House.[7] In "one of the greatest feats in house moving," the dilapidated wooden capitol was pushed westward to make way for the structure's foundations and to ensure that the General Assembly would continue to have a place to meet during construction.[8] A copy of Calhoun's final address to the US Senate "on the slavery question" was laid beneath the building's cornerstone in December 1851. Calhoun had delivered the speech weeks before his death, defending the constitutional rights of slaveholders, detailing the imbalance of power between North and South, and predicting that the North's "many aggressions" would destroy the Union.[9]

Cracks began to appear in the building's north wing the next year. The state engaged architects John Rudolph Niernsee (from Baltimore) and George Edward Walker (from Charleston) to replace Hammarskold, and although their relationship was contentious, both architects agreed that the state should abandon the unsound foundations and start over with an entirely new structure in 1854.[10] Governor John Lawrence Manning saw the "tearing down and uprooting" of the fireproof building as an opportunity for an even larger State House that would take full advantage of Columbia's wide avenues.[11] He reemphasized Governor Seabrook's suggestion to locate the building in the center of Main Street so that it could "be seen without obstruction from the four points of the compass and [would] present an appearance more dignified and imposing."[12]

Accordingly, the state consolidated the blocks between Assembly and Senate Streets and considered plans from both Niernsee and Walker for a monumental Classical Revival structure to rival the Tennessee State Capitol, then under construction in Nashville. Niernsee designed a cruciform building to take advantage of the new site at the center of Main Street, with temple-front porticos

John Rudolph Niernsee's design for the South Carolina State House,
early 1850s. Note his design for the tower and terraces, which were
never executed. Courtesy of Richland Library, Columbia, S.C.

balancing large wings for the House and Senate to either side. While he topped his building with a 180-foot-tall tower based on William Strickland's design for Tennessee's capitol, Walker suggested a magnificent dome. The state chose Niernsee's cheaper scheme with the more than $230,000 already wasted on the disastrous fireproof building in mind.[13]

The ceremonies dedicating the cornerstone of the new building in 1856 transferred the ideological intentions of the failed fireproof building to the new State House: with President Franklin Pierce in attendance, the cornerstone was laid atop yet another copy of Calhoun's 1850 address. Recognizing that the building might be "completed amid the clash of arms," the keynote speaker defended southern slaveholder's rights to enslave African Americans: "We stand upon the broad platform of the Constitution and the law. . . . All others are rebels and traitors."[14] The building's ambitious scale, Niernsee's sophisticated design, and a sculptural program by noted artist Henry Kirke Brown made it a strong assertion of the state's sovereignty and commitment to slavery.

The General Assembly hired foreign-born stonecutters and paid the owners of hundreds of enslaved African Americans to shoulder the project.[15] Legislators enthusiastically described the enslaved workers cutting twenty-ton granite blocks for the building's walls at the nearby Granby Quarry as "a train-like machine powered by 'a triple combination of propelling forces, for wit: art, nature, and negros.'"[16] By the time the walls of the State House reached the seventy-foot cornice line five years later in 1861, South Carolina had seceded from the Union, joined the Confederate States of America, and fired the first shots of the Civil War.[17]

Progress was slow and interrupted throughout the war, but the preparation of stone and the carving of the portico's immense Corinthian capitals and marble details continued until 1863.[18] Union forces aimed its cannons at the building—still without a roof—when they captured Columbia in February 1865. The siege damaged the new building on its north and west elevations, broke its sculpture and unfinished columns, and burned the old State House.[19] A newspaper reported, "[The State House] had before the war assumed

The State House after the burning of Columbia in February 1865.
Note the unfinished walls of the building, the Palmetto Monument,
and the materials strewn about the construction site.
Historic Columbia Collection, HCF 2009.3.1.

dimensions and given tokens of the rare taste displayed in its construction, which had elicited the warmest encomiums of the critic and traveller. But to-day it stands chief among the monumental ruins of Columbia, an emblem eloquent with unuttered curses upon Sherman and his horde."[20]

A temporary roof and other repairs allowed the Reconstruction-era General Assembly to occupy the new State House for the first time in 1869.[21] Elected under federal occupation, this government was Republican and the only African American–majority state legislature in American history.[22] Interiors were outfitted for immediate use, but the state's postwar economic devastation prevented the building's completion or even proper upkeep. Following the end of Reconstruction with the reinstatement of a White, Democratic majority, the state rehired Niernsee in 1885 to complete the building as inexpensively as possible.

Niernsee died unexpectedly, and the state pivoted to his Baltimore-based partner, J. Crawford Neilson, to supervise the installation of a new roof and the completion of the exterior granite walls and wooden interiors (including a lobby ceiling painted an eye-popping blue). To save money amid a collapsed economy, the leg-

Stereograph of the State House with its temporary roof in the early 1870s. Historic Columbia Collection, HCF 2005.8.2.

The State House ca. 1895, before the dome and porticos were
completed. Note the location of the George Washington monument,
which occupied the spot briefly held by the Confederate Monument
after it was moved to its current location. Courtesy of
Richland Library, Columbia, S.C.

islature delayed the construction of the porticos; ignored Neilson's
suggestions for adding extra stories; and relied on forced labor from
unskilled, impoverished African American convicts.[23]

Amid public accusations of corruption in 1888, the state replaced
Neilson with Frank McHenry Niernsee, the son of the building's antebellum architect.[24] Niernsee installed the capitol's first plumbing
and electrical systems and replaced the recently completed wooden
interiors with fireproof materials, including the surviving cast-iron
library and "massive, yet attractive" lobby stair.[25] The state again
halted funding for the project by the early 1890s, leaving Niernsee's
designs for the State House's porticos and tower unfinished once
again.[26]

Facing pressure from constituents who were frustrated that
"money enough has been thrown away in patching up the building to almost finish it," the General Assembly hired local architect
Frank Pierce Milburn in 1900 to complete the porticos, interiors,

The State House in 1905, shortly after its completion with
Milburn's dome. Courtesy of South Caroliniana Library,
University of South Carolina, Columbia, S.C.

and crowning feature on a shoestring budget.[27] Milburn, who had
already designed courthouses, train stations, and campus buildings throughout the New South, was eager for such a prestigious
commission.[28] To appeal to the cash-strapped state, he proposed a
metal and wood dome-within-a-dome rather than Niernsee's now
fifty-year-old design for a granite tower.[29] The solution squared with
many of the Beaux-Arts-inspired State Houses then under construction, including those for Rhode Island, Georgia, and Pennsylvania.
The South Carolina State House was finally declared completed in
1903, more than fifty years after the laying of its cornerstone.

Confronting engineering reports that declared Milburn's dome
unsafe, the state immediately turned around and sued the architect
for shoddy craftmanship and deficient engineering. The legislature refused to take responsibility for hamstringing his work with a
meager appropriation. Calls to replace the "simply infamous" dome
began immediately, but public sentiment ensured that such would
only happen when "the pockets of the people are so well lined that

they can gratify their aesthetic taste."[30] The legislature hired local architect Charles C. Wilson to address "difficulties in construction, as well as taste in architectural design," but the legislature was never willing to pay to replace Milburn's dome.[31] For decades to come, many refused to consider the building "completed" and continued to advocate for the construction of a new dome or Niernsee's original tower design.[32]

The State House's inadequate square footage continued to be a problem throughout the twentieth century regardless of disagreements over the tastefulness of the dome. Legislators and architects regularly suggested expanding the building with wings or rearranging its interiors. Fortunately, concerns over spending taxpayer money to continually "fix" the beleaguered State House—as well as devotion to Niernsee's original design—encouraged the construction of stand-alone state office buildings instead. The construction of the Calhoun Building (1926), Hampton Building (1938), and Capitol Complex (1970s) relieved the cramped State House and preserved its singular drama at the center of the grounds. The interiors have been renovated multiple times, most recently with earthquake-proofing and a restoration of the Milburn and Frank Niernsee interiors in the 1990s.

Swanson Lunsford Grave

Buried 1799; markers erected 1837, 1953

The grave of Swanson Lunsford (1750s–99) is the earliest monument on the State House grounds and perhaps its most mysterious. Born in Petersburg, Virginia, Lunsford came to South Carolina under the command of Light Horse Harry Lee and Nathanael Greene during the Revolutionary War. He married into a prominent local family and became one of the city's earliest commissioners in charge "of the streets and markets of the town."[33] Lunsford died in July 1799 after

Swanson Lunsford's Grave. Photograph by Chandler Yonkers, 2020.

contracting yellow fever in Charleston and was buried on what was then the southwest corner of the State House grounds.[34]

There are many explanations for why Lunsford is the only person buried at the state capitol. Disproven or unlikely theories include that his family or friends owned the land at the time of his death, that he was an important public official with impressive military service, or that he was from out of state and thus had no family churchyard to take his body.[35] The most probable reason is that officials feared the potential of his body to spread yellow fever in a churchyard or public cemetery.[36]

In 1837 Lunsford's daughter petitioned the state legislature to build a "humble monument to his memory" at the grave, suggesting that it was previously unmarked.[37] The state agreed to install a marker that read: "Capt. Swanson Lunsford, a native of Virginia, and for many years a resident of Columbia: died Aug. 7th, 1799, aged about forty years. He was a member of Lee's Legion in the eventful period of 1776. This humble tribute to his memory has been placed by his only children, Mrs. M. L. and her husband, Dr. John Douglass, of Chester, SC."[38] The explicit mention of his military service hints at the nation's renewed reverence for the passing Revolutionary generation in the 1830s.[39]

The grave endured periods of neglect over the late nineteenth and early twentieth centuries, offering a testament to the state's inability or unwillingness to properly maintain the grounds. The *State* newspaper wistfully remarked in 1899: "Few know of the existence of the grave, and fewer still know its story. For Time, the tomb-builder, has taken away the contemporaries of the one interred."[40] Renewed attention to the grounds at the time of the Hampton Monument's installation in 1906 prompted the state to remove a large oak tree that shaded the grave and to repair its enclosure.[41]

Lunsford's twentieth-century descendants resumed interest in the grave as part of a larger trend among middle- and upper-class White Americans to research and memorialize their genealogies (this movement also resulted in the erection of the Partisan Generals Monument by the Daughters of the American Revolution on the opposite side of the grounds in 1913). The Sons of the American Revolution cleaned up the grave in 1924, and Lunsford's great-grandson (also a member of the organization) installed a medallion identifying Lunsford as a Revolutionary soldier in 1927.[42] Lunsford's great-great-granddaughter, Mary Craig Baker, commissioned the current stone to surround and transcribe the illegible original in 1953.[43] Archaeological investigation has never been conducted to confirm that this is the site of Lunsford's grave.

George Washington Monument

Purchased 1858

William James Hubard, after Jean-Antoine Houdon

South Carolina's statue of the Revolutionary War general and America's first president, George Washington (1732–99), is a full-size bronze copy of a marble sculpture by Jean-Antoine Houdon made for the Virginia State Capitol in 1788–92. Purchased by South Carolina for its new capitol building in 1858, the statue of the iconic planter asserted the state's arguments for the righteousness of slavery and its resistance against federal power. The statue set the tone for the antebellum sculptural program begun one year later by Henry Kirke Brown and continued in the twentieth century with the bronze figures of Wade Hampton, Benjamin Tillman, Jimmy Byrnes, and Strom Thurmond.

Guided by Thomas Jefferson, Virginia commissioned the most famous French sculptor of the Enlightenment to depict Washington in a novel composition: Houdon's work was both a faithful portrait and an allegorical representation of Washington as the ancient Roman general Cincinnatus. The comparison between Washington and Cincinnatus was extremely popular in the eighteenth and early nineteenth centuries. Washington's compatriots praised him for relinquishing power to elected bodies after the Revolution rather than choosing to rule as a despot, just as Cincinnatus had refused to be emperor after a military victory. Washington wears his uniform as commander of the Continental Army, but the plow at his feet suggests the civilian life to which he returned after resigning in 1783. His sword and cape hang on the bundled thirteen rods of a Roman fasces, representing the power of the union of former colonies to which he deferred. Based on Houdon's life mask of Washington, the work was quickly regarded as the best likeness of Washington and the finest example of sculpture in the United States.[44]

The Virginia state legislature granted exclusive permission to the enterprising English-born painter James William Hubard to copy the Houdon sculpture in 1853.[45] Washington was an especially popular figure throughout the South in the years leading up to the Civil War. Southerners challenging the federal government over the issue of slavery saw themselves as the second coming of the American Revolution, and Virginia was particularly interested in laying claim to Washington's memory. In the same years the state also commissioned a new bronze equestrian statue of Washington for its capitol grounds.[46] The destruction of a neoclassical sculpture of the first president by Italian artist Antonio Canova in an 1831 fire at the North Carolina State Capitol had many wary of the potential loss of the Houdon.[47] Promoters hoped that by distributing faithful copies

Jean-Antoine Houdon's statue of George Washington in the Virginia State Capitol. Library of Congress, Prints & Photographs Division, Detroit Publishing Company Collection.

of Houdon's sculpture, the work could be admired nationwide as well.[48]

Hubard began the costly and difficult process of making molds and plaster casts in the summer of 1853. With bronze casting in its infancy in the United States, his Richmond foundry was one of only a handful in the country.[49] As noted in a newspaper account: "There were no experienced men of Munich in our country to mix and melt and mould the metal; and to make the section molds, such as Italians use, was itself almost an art." It ultimately took Hubard three years to successfully produce six full-size bronze copies of the Houdon sculpture.[50] But he projected that every state in the nation would want one and that the work could lead to a commission for a monumental sculpture of Washington at Mount Vernon, predicting a substantial return on his investment and labor.[51] To drum up interest, he displayed his plaster casts of the statue at the Crystal Palace in London, in New York City, and at the US Capitol.[52] The outbreak of the Civil War prevented Hubard from producing more copies. After switching to munitions production for the Confederacy and with his finances in ruins, he died from injuries sustained after a shell exploded in his foundry in 1862.[53] Copying the Houdon sculpture in bronze would not be attempted again until the twentieth century.[54]

The South Carolina legislature purchased one of Hubard's six bronzes for $10,000 over 1857–58, making it the state's first investment in public art for its new state house then under construction.[55] As a slaveholder who defied the British Crown, Washington made an especially attractive symbol for the planter-politicians claiming sovereignty from the federal government in South Carolina. A Charleston newspaper said of the purchase: "could anything be more consonant with the feelings of this community, which has ever cherished with pride the manners and institutions of our revolutionary period, than to have in our midst, and in perpetuity, the statue of him, who, even amid the purity and simplicity of that era of our Republic, stood pre-eminent. The time is propitious."[56] Soon after South Carolina's purchase of the Hubard bronze, the new equestrian statue of Washington in Richmond appeared on the seal of the Confederacy, and Jefferson Davis was inaugurated as its president at the statue's base on Washington's birthday, February 22, 1862.[57]

After traveling from Richmond to the port of Charleston, South Carolina's Houdon copy remained in storage until the new capitol was sufficiently completed to house it.[58] By the time of the 1865 burning of Columbia, the statue was in place on the first floor of the building. It was first moved outside in front of the State House in 1889. Sitting atop a base constructed of scrap marble by convict laborers, it sat across from the Palmetto Monument and centered on the building's east side (it took the place of the Confederate Monument, which had moved from that location to its current spot on

Washington statue with plaque (installed 1930), broken cane,
and base (made 1911) at the bottom of the State House steps.
Photograph by Chandler Yonkers, 2020.

Gervais Street in 1884). The erection of new monuments (including those for Wade Hampton and the partisan generals) and a new
wave of Houdon bronzes finally convinced the legislature to autho-
rize a new location and pedestal in the first decade of the twentieth century.[59] The renewed statue was placed at the bottom of the
State House steps in 1911 so that "to the artistic eye, Washington will
then appear as having just descended the steps to the esplanade and
paused to view the surroundings."[60]

The statue's broken cane has long generated discussion. In his oft-
quoted account of the 1865 burning of Columbia, William Gilmore
Simms reported that at the hands of federal soldiers, Washington's
figure "received several bruises from brickbats, addressed to face and
breast. A shell scratched his back, and the staff which he bore in his
hand was broken in the middle."[61] At the height of criticism about
the Reconstruction-era African American legislature, other stories
blamed unruly Black citizens for the broken cane as evidence of

Black men's unfitness for power.[62] State historian Alexander Salley tried to repair the cane in 1908, but the replacement part "made and fitted into the grooves and socket of the original cane" later broke off.[63]

Likely prompted by the 1932 bicentennial of George Washington's birth and as part of the campaign to recognize other injuries caused to the site during the burning of Columbia (including the first State House marker and stars on the side of the State House), Alexander Salley affixed a bronze tablet to the statue in 1930. The choice to leave the cane broken and to definitively blame the "federal soldiers" for their "abuse" in the plaque's text precluded any attempts to obscure the evidence with a repair in the future.[64]

Sculpture on the North Façade of the State House

Installed 1859–61
Henry Kirke Brown

Nationally renowned neoclassical sculptor Henry Kirke Brown designed and partially executed the State House's marble decorative program in 1859–61. His pairs of cameo portraits, eagles in constellations of stars, and fasces were installed just before the Civil War halted work on the building. He also designed massive allegorical figures and images of enslaved African Americans for the State House's pediment, but the Civil War terminated the project.

State House architect John Rudolph Niernsee hired Brown in the spring of 1859 to sculpt two profile portraits for the building's north façade. He fueled the artist's hopes that the job would expand to a "very large work . . . more worthy of [his] chisel": a scene that would fill the pediment of the one-hundred-foot-long north portico.[65] Despite receiving high praise for his recently unveiled equestrian statue of George Washington in New York City, Brown was desperate for work. His finances were in shambles and his ego bruised after his design for the US Capitol's pediment was rejected in part for including an African American figure.[66] Regarding Niernsee's design for the State House "in better taste than the US Capitol," Brown accepted the commission as the next-best job in American sculpture.[67]

Flanking the building's main entrance, Brown's marble portraits depicted the recently deceased state politicians George McDuffie (1790–1851) and Robert Young Hayne (1791–1839), staunch advocates of slavery and nullification alongside John C. Calhoun in the 1830s. It is unclear who decided to feature these two men in particular, but their politics remained popular in the 1850s. Governor William Henry Gist quoted McDuffie in his 1859 address to the General Assembly, using his words to defend South Carolina's right to secede from the Union over slavery: "Let us cherish and preserve

Henry Kirke Brown's sculptures on the north side of the State House. Photograph by Chandler Yonkers, 2020.

the reputation we have nobly acquired, as the Romans did their ves-tal fire."[68] The choice of McDuffie, a self-made lawyer from the up-country, and Hayne, a member of the Lowcountry's planter class, also signaled the importance of unity among White South Carolin-ians in the face of the federal government's supposed oppression.[69] Depicted in togas and as cameos, a technique originating in ancient Greece, the portraits suggest the timelessness of their beliefs.[70]

Brown also directed and likely finished the carving of the pairs of eagles and fasces below the portraits. Set in fields of stars, the eagles are adaptations of the Great Seal of the United States.[71] Their faces turn toward the olive branches clutched in their talons, which rep-resent peace, and away from the arrows, which represent war. The fasces beneath the eagles are an ancient symbol of unity and govern-ment, echoing the bundle of rods in the Houdon sculpture (recently purchased by the state and with which Brown was very familiar).[72] Some have attributed the coordinating number of fifteen stars and rods to the number of potential states of the Confederacy and claimed that the building was intended as "the Capitol of a Southern Confederacy, already looming on the political horizon."[73] But the timing of key events in the development of the war and the work's federal symbolism suggests this is an unlikely explanation.[74]

The state was so pleased with Brown's work that it retained him —just as he had hoped—to plan sculpture for the building's north pediment. He designed an unorthodox composition of twelve fig-ures to fill the triangular format. He depicted eight African Ameri-cans on either side of ten-foot-tall female representations of Hope,

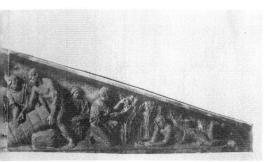

Henry Kirke Brown's plaster model for the sculptures on the State House pediment, which was destroyed in the burning of Columbia. Henry Kirke Bush-Brown Papers, Manuscript Division, Library of Congress.

An unidentified worker with Brown's plaster model for the figure of Hope, which would have occupied the center of the State House pediment. Henry Kirke Bush-Brown Papers, Manuscript Division, Library of Congress.

Justice, and Liberty.[75] The muscular Black male figures picked cotton, harvested rice, and relaxed in classical poses in fields, supervised by a White overseer on a horse and assisted by a Black woman with a basket. Unlike earlier representations of enslaved people, the pediment idealized enslaved laborers and pictured them without chains or caricature.[76]

People on either side of the slavery debate read Brown's design in different ways. Abolitionists (including Brown's friends and family), saw in the laboring figures a statement of slavery's "degraded humanity," a condemnation of cash crops' destruction of the southern soil, and an underhanded argument for abolition.[77] Slavery's advocates saw it as an affirmation of the institution's righteousness. One newspaper exclaimed, "The figures of the negros are excellent, displaying their race in marked [contrast] with the refined and intellectual figures of the central group of the Anglo-Saxon race."[78]

The work—and Brown—embodied the paradoxes of 1860s America. By the start of the war, he came to see slavery as a "self destroying blight" and believed that "without the destruction of Slavery there can be no general prosperity in the South," yet he and his wife had socialized often with prominent slaveholders (including Calhoun's relatives) during their time living in Columbia.[79] While it is tempting to see Brown's pediment as an attempt to trick South Carolinians into accepting a design that celebrated the labor of enslaved people, it is more likely that the ambitious artist intended his design to be ambiguous enough to please his clients, bring him national attention, and fit within his own beliefs. Since his initial proposal to include an enslaved man on the pediment of the US Capitol, it is probable that he was also fully exploiting the prominent opportunity to recognize enslaved peoples' humanity in slavery's hotbed.[80]

Despite such high hopes, Brown's progress on the sculptural program was slow over his two years in South Carolina. He broke his arm and suffered various other accidents and illnesses; the clamors of war were distracting; and he and his wife felt stifled, both by the southern heat and the incendiary political climate.[81] After finishing the eagles, fasces, portraits, pediment models, and a plaster version of Hope, he abandoned his Columbia studio and fled north in the spring of 1861—just months after the Confederacy's attack on Fort Sumter.[82] All of his pediment models were destroyed in the burning of Columbia in February 1865, but thankfully after they had been photographed. The building's north portico was finished with a blank pediment in 1903.

Palmetto Monument

Erected 1854
Christopher Werner, with later changes and additions

The story of the twenty-foot-tall Palmetto Monument is unusually long and complex. Sculptor Christopher Werner took advantage of an indecisive legislature and made the cast-iron, copper, and bronze

Palmetto Monument. Photograph by Chandler Yonkers, 2020.

palmetto tree to commemorate South Carolina's Mexican-American War dead on speculation in the early 1850s. The palmetto tree (or *sabal palmetto*) had appeared on the state seal since the eighteenth century and inspired the name of the infantry regiment of volunteers—the Palmetto Regiment—from South Carolina that fought in the war.

Typical of the decorative ironwork popular in the mid-nineteenth century, it combines Greek Revival stylistic elements (such as the large acanthus leaves at the base of the tree's trunk) with more Romantic ones (including the fanciful scrollwork and crowns on the enclosure's posts). Its clever combination of materials ensured that the copper fronds would turn green over time, making the tree appear even more lifelike. It is the first war monument erected on the State House grounds and one of the earliest of the few Mexican-American War monuments built in the United States.

The Mexican-American War was fought in 1846–48 over territory in what is now Texas, California, Nevada, Utah, New Mexico, Arizona, Colorado, Oklahoma, Kansas, and Wyoming. America's victory and subsequent annexation of land greatly increased the country's size and inflamed debates over the political balance between states that allowed slavery and those that did not. South Carolina eagerly participated in the war because a win would ensure the westward expansion of slavery and the power of slave states in Congress. Led by former governor Pierce Mason Butler, South Carolina's Palmetto Regiment suffered a higher percentage of deaths than any other American unit in the conflict; almost half of the regiment's soldiers died.[83]

Soon after Butler's death in the Battle of Churubusco in 1847 (and before the end of the war), the South Carolina legislature agreed that "something must be done, and done liberally." Legislators proposed pensions and medals for veterans and their families and resolved to erect a monument "on some suitable site in the town of Columbia" to commemorate "this gallant and devoted regiment."[84] The legislature approached Charleston architect Edward Brickell White to propose a design. He conceived an "original, striking and grand" tomb for the regiment's dead enclosed in a pyramid of "natural rocks" and topped by a thirty-five-foot tall bronze allegorical trophy consisting of an urn, eagle, rattle snake, and the regiment's banners. A giant bronze palmetto tree passed through the entire granite pyramid and emerged from its peak, recalling the name of the regiment and the image on the state's seal. But the legislature balked at the monument's $25,000 price and the project languished.[85]

Frustrated by the state's inaction, the regiment's veterans and their families began a private campaign to build a monument by 1851.[86] They planned at the very least to erect a marker over the remains of Pierce Butler (the only member of the regiment whose body was returned to the United States) that would also recognize the sacrifice of the entire regiment.[87] But by 1853 Butler's family had disinterred his body from its temporary grave in Trinity churchyard and moved it to its permanent resting place in the family graveyard in Saluda, South Carolina.[88]

Without Butler's remains, clear direction from the legislature, or even a specific site, the project seemed hopeless until Christopher Werner saw an opportunity. While at work on the new State House's ironwork (now lost), the enterprising artist made and erected a cast-iron palmetto tree on the south side of the building at his own expense in 1854. With the tree already installed, he hoped that the state would pay him for it and dedicate it to the veterans.[89] It is possible that Werner either imagined that his tree could be incorporated into White's proposed pyramid in the future or that White's design inspired the novel design.

A German immigrant and colorful local figure, Werner had first opened a blacksmith shop in Charleston in the 1830s or '40s. He fed the port city's taste for the latest fashions in decorative ironwork (surviving examples of which include the Sword Gates at 32 Legare Street and the railing surrounding Randolph Hall at the College of Charleston).[90] Werner owned twelve enslaved individuals and hired slaves from other masters, making it likely that enslaved craftsmen contributed to the Palmetto Monument.[91]

The state finally purchased the tree from Werner two years after its erection for $5,000, satisfying a public that was growing increasingly frustrated as the war's veterans continued to pass away without a monument.[92] The legislature then commissioned Werner to make plaques listing the names of the regiment's soldiers with raised, gilt bronze letters and a "bronzed eagle" for the top of the tree (perhaps recalling White's design). But problems arose immediately: some of the names were misspelled, the welded letters began to fall off, an eagle was deemed "inappropriate" for the design, and the legislature refused to pay Werner for the additional labor. The artist made and installed new markers and a "palmetto cabbage" on top of the tree but was never paid the full $11,000 he claimed the project had cost him to produce.[93] The various fonts on the monument's three plaques indicate that they continued to be edited well into the twentieth century.

A relatively fragile sculpture, the Palmetto Monument has suffered multiple injuries. "Sherman's vandals" supposedly carried off two of the plaques during the February 1865 destruction of the grounds, necessitating their replacement.[94] The decorative cast iron

The Palmetto Monument in its original configuration, ca. 1877. Courtesy of Richland Library, Columbia, S.C.

surround Werner made for the monument was separated from the palmetto tree in the 1870s, and the posts were not reunited until a hundred years later. The frilly arches that connected the posts have long been lost, and the current chains are twentieth-century replacements.[95] Hurricanes and tornadoes have damaged the monument, breaking and bending its fronds.[96] A 1939 tornado knocked the tree from its base, and subsequent repairs by craftsmen funded by the Works Progress Administration revealed that Werner had numbered the fronds and trunk so that each could be reinstalled in its appropriate place.[97] In 1874 the monument was moved from the south side of the capitol to the front.[98] When the Confederate Monument was erected in front of the east wing four years later, the Palmetto Monument was centered on the building's west wing, where it sat until it was moved to its current location in 1972.[99]

⟪ TWO ⟫

Jim Crow and the State House Beautiful (1877–1968)

Begun as a monument to slave-holding South Carolinians' power, the unfinished capitol emerged from the Civil War as a stark reminder of the federal government's victory and the subsequent abolition of slavery. After Democrats won the state elections of 1876, ending Reconstruction, they reclaimed the meaning of the battered State House and grounds. White South Carolinians made the site the proving ground for their "redemption" of the state's identity from "black supremacy," "carpetbaggers," and emancipated and politically empowered African Americans.[1] These "redeemers" exploited the State House's symbolism as they resumed the building's construction, passed laws that restricted Blacks' civil rights, and rebuilt the war-torn state over the next seventy-five years.

Although legislators were deeply invested in the ideological power of the State House grounds, generation after generation hesitated or refused to appropriate funding to improve them. Since the state's inception, the ambivalence toward funding public monuments and architecture had clashed with the recognition of their potential to bolster their politics and values. This left groups of private citizens—often composed exclusively of women—to create most of the monuments built in South Carolina's symbolic center.

Despite tensions between the legislature's frugality and the popularity of monuments, the State House and grounds expanded with two new state office buildings and more than a dozen new monuments in the century following the building's first occupation in 1869. The John C. Calhoun and Wade Hampton Buildings tripled the government's square footage and led the way for the grounds' expansion south of Senate Street. The state government and private groups blended memories of the Civil War and Reconstruction in monuments related to one another through visual sight lines and expressive rhetoric. The redeemers' historical narrative and political power went unchallenged until the 1950s and 1960s, when African Americans protested segregation, voter suppression, and racial violence on the grounds and the federal government began enforcing civil rights legislation.

Plans for the State House Landscape

Designed and executed 1878
Edward Otto Schwagerl, landscape architect

Designed 1904–5
Harlan P. Kelsey, landscape architect

Over the century between the end of the Civil War and the construction of the Capitol Complex south of Senate Street in 1969–81, the State House grounds fluctuated between being the subject of intense scrutiny and the victim of the legislature's disinterest in spending taxpayer money on public works. Periods of neglect alternated with improvements prompted by renewed attention from major anniversaries or the installation of new monuments. Throughout this turbulent century, South Carolinians believed strongly in the potential of the State House's setting to make connections between their past, present, and future.

Like most public buildings in America of the eighteenth and early nineteenth centuries, Columbia's first State House was not initially set in a designed landscape. But by the 1840s, visitors who found the old building "a disgrace to the Palmetto State" could at least enjoy a "romantic garden" and nursery planted by amateur horticulturalist Robert Russell across Main Street.[2] They marveled at its "innumerable varieties of rare and beautiful plants," "lofty magnolias," "serpentine paths," "tempting fruits," and elaborate fountains.[3] By 1846 Russell had expanded his attention to the capitol building, laying out graveled walks, planting trees, and even cultivating tea plants, as the State House grounds' first official superintendent.[4] All of Russell's work was destroyed a decade later when the state abandoned the foundations of the fireproof building and decided to build a new State House at the center of Main Street. The granite walls of the building's east wing stretched across the land formerly shaded by Russell's arbors.[5]

The Civil War and the capitol's stop-and-start construction process prevented serious consideration of walkways or plantings on the expanded two-block grounds over the next two decades. The first legislatures to occupy the building during Reconstruction remarked frequently on the "dilapidated condition and unseemly appearance" of the area but could focus their short tenures only on making the building itself habitable.[6] Until the late 1870s the Palmetto Monument and Lunsford grave marker stood isolated in a construction site scattered with "rubbish and obstacles" such as broken columns, outhouses, sheds, and falling-down fences.[7]

The "redemption" government of Wade Hampton (1877–79) was the first in the state's history to envision the grounds as a park with a comprehensive plan. Executed in the late 1870s and respected by Robert Marvin's 1969 redesign, the plan's system of paths still is recognizable to today's visitors. In 1878 the state commissioned "perfectly beautiful and generally approved" drawings from German-born landscape architect Edward Otto Schwagerl.[8] Schwagerl had designed parks, cemeteries, and campuses in the popular picturesque style throughout the United States and would later settle in the Pacific northwest.[9] A working drawing in the South Carolina Department of Archives and History based on Schwagerl's design lays out paths and specifies grading and drainage for the site.[10] Following a similar hierarchical system of paths as Frederick Law Olmsted's celebrated Central Park in New York City (built in the 1850s), the drawing separates different kinds of traffic. A wide carriage drive connects the north and south fronts (the porticos would go unfinished until the early twentieth century) to either side of Main Street and rings around the building, while a narrower pedestrian path follows the perimeter of the blocks and bridges a kidney-shaped drainage pond in the northwest corner (where the Sims Monument now sits). The plan's symmetrical organization respects the classical symmetry of the State House's architecture, but its graceful lines

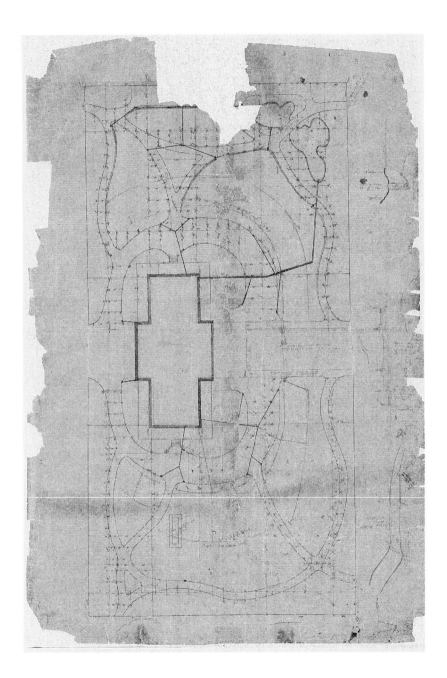

provide a contrast in keeping with the Romantic ideals of the nineteenth century. In 1878 convicts began laying the curved gravel walks according to the drawing, planted trees and shrubs, and dug a lake deep enough "to drown almost any unhappy man."[11] Wade Hampton provided a young alligator to live in the pond, no doubt delighting (or terrifying) the visitors who soon found the grounds "quite a popular afternoon promenade."[12]

Although Schwagerl's plan did not suggest locations for future monuments, the "redeemers" added a constellation of monuments to the renewed public space. Updating the goals of Henry Kirke Brown's antebellum sculptural program for a new era, Democratic politicians and private groups increasingly saw the grounds as an opportunity to celebrate the Confederacy, the state's sovereignty over federal power, and their reclamation of the government from the state's African American majority. Immediately following Hampton's ousting of the Reconstruction-era Republicans, one supporter pronounced: "It would be well for us to rear a bronze column on the State House grounds at Columbia, to commemorate our deliverance from the rule of the stranger."[13] Such monuments would be in line with those built on Monument Avenue in Richmond, Virginia, and on capitol and courthouse squares across the South in the 1870s–1920s. Often called the "Lost Cause," their perspective on the Civil War rationalized secession with a heroic view of the antebellum South and insisted that southerners had been defending their constitutional rights and way of life rather than slavery.[14] By linking monuments together along sight lines, South Carolinians connected southern Whites' return to power with this emerging interpretation of the Civil War and the state's colonial and antebellum history.[15] To accomplish this, the legislature positioned the Confederate and Palmetto Monuments on either side of the State House in 1878–79, moved the Confederate Monument in front of the building in 1884, and placed the George Washington statue opposite the Palmetto in 1889.

Facing: Plan for the State House grounds, ca. 1878,
likely by (or after) Edward Otto Schwagerl.
South Carolina Department of Archives and History.

By 1900 the park looked worse for wear. The *State* reported that "the grass is deep and ragged; white, yellow and red clover crop out in tufts here and there, vetch and lupines run riot till the convicts come to cut them down."[16] The national obsession with civic improvement, the commissioning of the grounds' first monument in decades, and the long-awaited completion of the building heightened embarrassment over the state of the grounds. Columbia's White citizens pressured state legislators to remedy the situation, prompting a new wave of monument building and master planning.

Within months of the completion of the State House dome, many hoped that Columbia would join the City Beautiful movement, then "being pushed in every part of the country."[17] Cities across America were building new parks, improving sanitary systems, paving roads, and investing in civic art and architecture as part of comprehensive urban plans. Architects remade downtown Chicago and the National Mall in Washington and offered dazzling visions of perfect cities at world's fairs.[18] In response, elite women formed the Civic Improvement League and hired Boston-based landscape architecture firm Kelsey & Guild to devise a master plan for Columbia in 1904.[19] Harlan P. Kelsey delivered a lengthy illustrated report the next year that praised the city's "Magnificent Streets" and made particular recommendations for its mill villages, trees, and drainage issues.[20]

Kelsey's comprehensive plan focused considerable attention on the area around the State House. Responding to the need for convenient office space for the government's growing bureaucracy, he suggested that by arranging any new buildings "around an open space or mall, the dignity and architectural importance of each building is enhanced by those around it, while the larger group forms a unit which can be treated with proper regard for architectural effect and in a manner commensurate with its civic importance." Recognizing that "Capitol Park will always be one of the most invaluable breathing spots in the city," he warned that "this park should be properly laid out and cared for by the state, and only in this way will it ever become a fitting place for the chief building of the state." He offered two Beaux-Arts-inspired schemes that located large buildings along Main and Senate Streets and specified that they should be in "a style agreeing with the Capitol."[21]

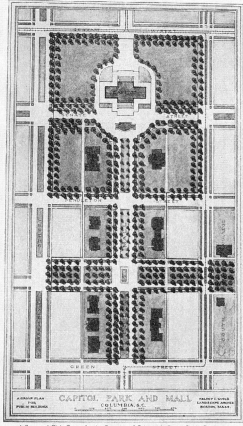

Harlan P. Kelsey's master plan for the expansion of the State House grounds, 1905. Courtesy of HathiTrust.

Although Kelsey's plan was never fully realized (few City Beautiful plans were), it did galvanize enthusiasm for the city's improvement and guided future development of the grounds. Following his suggestions, subsequent legislatures "jealously guarded" the State House from additions and constructed new buildings along the underdeveloped southern stretch of Main Street: first with the Calhoun, Hampton, and Highway Buildings along Senate Street in the 1920s–50s, and later within the Capitol Complex pedestrian mall of the 1970s.[22] With the exception of the International Style Highway Building (built in 1952 and renovated with a Brutalist skin in the

1970s), the architects of each of these office buildings used classical proportions and principles that complemented the State House.

Another outsider with national clout, French sculptor Frederick Wellington Ruckstull, advised Columbia on achieving the City Beautiful in the same years.[23] A state-appointed commission (influenced by the women of the Civic Improvement League) first brought Ruckstull to Columbia to sculpt the statue of Wade Hampton for the capitol grounds in 1904. He buoyed White citizens already deeply committed to celebrating the Lost Cause and the post-Reconstruction "redemption," telling the Civic Improvement League: "Regeneration and prosperity are in the air in the South, and all you need is to get together, lift up your heads and hold aloft the banner of city embellishment, and constantly follow that ideal."[24] The city's elite invited the sculptor to visit Columbia many times over the following decades, elevating him to celebrity status and soliciting his advice on all things artistic. Ruckstull ultimately designed three sculptures for the State House grounds—the Hampton, Confederate Women's, and Partisan Generals Monuments—as well as the marble statues of Hampton (1929) and John C. Calhoun (1910) that continue to represent the state in the US Capitol.[25]

Columbians unveiled Ruckstull's Hampton Monument in the fall of 1906, with Kelsey's ideas still fresh in their minds. The poor state of the grounds was on full view for the thousands of visitors who came to the ceremony, prompting the *State* to remark: "Think of setting a three million dollar building and these beautiful monuments in the middle of an old field or of a cow pasture! The 'sidewalks' girding the grounds are nothing but uncurbed, unpaved footpaths. Paths bisect the grass plots; there are a few hundred feet of gas-pipe railing."[26] Following a reproach by the governor on the grounds' "disgraceful condition," the General Assembly appointed a new commission and appropriated $15,000 for their improvement. The amount was still "entirely too small to undertake to carry out the original plans of a cut-stone retaining wall around the terrace" for the building as designed by John Rudolph Niernsee, but new beds were planted, and walks replenished so that "South Carolina may and can advertise herself to the world."[27]

The secretary of state and various commissions continued to improve the grounds with intermittent bursts of funding over the following decades.[28] But a lack of adequate or consistent commitment to the property allowed plenty of room for interventions made without much consideration or discussion. New sidewalks were added according to visitors' well-worn paths rather than any adherence to the 1878 plan.[29] Walks were paved only in sections and with varying materials, trees and beds planted and replaced willy-nilly, and monuments vandalized. Problems associated with vehicles increased with the number of state employees and their rising expectations for convenient parking. Legislators perennially voted down rules introduced to "prohibit driving or carrying horses or mules across any grounds," and by the 1920s they began to park cars around the Confederate Monument.[30] The condition of the grounds—and especially the "excess of wantonly parked vehicles" around the Confederate Monument—motivated a major rehabilitation and master plan for the State House grounds by the 1960s.[31]

South Carolina Monument to the Confederate Dead (Confederate Monument)

Unveiled 1879
Muldoon, Walton & Company, manufacturer

Sculpture replaced 1884
Carlo Nicoli, sculptor

The South Carolina Monument to the Confederate Dead dominates the north side of the State House grounds. The marble obelisk topped by a lone soldier, typical of Lost Cause monuments, was the first monument to be erected on the State House grounds following

South Carolina Monument to the Confederate Dead. Photograph by Chandler Yonkers, 2020.

Reconstruction.[32] Its 1879 unveiling celebrated White South Carolinians' "redemption."

In 1869 a group of White women formed the South Carolina Monument Association (SCMA) to commemorate the Confederate dead and resist the biracial state government.[33] Because the African American, Republican-majority legislature was unlikely to permit such a monument on the State House grounds, the group purchased a site on Taylor's Hill near the governor's mansion.[34] The poor quality of the site's soil soon forced the SCMA to accept a new site in Elmwood Cemetery.[35]

The South Carolina Monument to the Confederate Dead in its original location against the State House with its original sculpture, ca. 1879. Courtesy of South Caroliniana Library, University of South Carolina, Columbia, S.C.

By 1873 the SCMA had raised enough money to order a carved obelisk and statue of Italian marble from Muldoon, Walton & Company.[36] Commemorating all of South Carolina's Confederate dead, the monument was a very early example of a type commissioned for civic spaces in both the North and the South following the Civil War.[37] In contrast to monuments dedicated to individuals like the equestrian statue of Wade Hampton, such sculptures idealized the sacrifice, self-restraint, and morality of the common soldier.[38] The inscription by William Henry Trescot evoked soldiers' connections to the families they had left at home, including the very women who raised funds for the monument.[39]

Although it had already built a granite base for the obelisk in Elmwood Cemetery, the SCMA petitioned the legislature for a site on the State House grounds once Democrats had overthrown the Republican-led state government. Governor Wade Hampton's new Democratic administration heartily agreed and erected the monument along the east wing of the State House opposite the Palmetto Monument. Masons placed Confederate flags, money, and a copy of the Order of Secession in the cornerstone, and ten thousand people attended the unveiling in the spring of 1879.[40] The *State* newspaper later described the memorial's dual commemoration of Lost Cause and post-Reconstruction "redemption": "The monument therefore stands not only as a memorial to the men who fought for southern rights, but as a testimonial to the courage of the women whose noble endeavors in days darker than war itself were persevered until their labors were crowned with success."[41]

Three years after its unveiling, a lightning strike decapitated the figure "as if by a guillotine" and damaged the obelisk. Columbia women immediately raised money for a new, slightly different sculpture by Carlo Nicoli.[42] The state reinstalled the revised monument on axis with Main Street and the State House in 1884 and moved the statue of George Washington outside and in front of the capitol's east wing a few years later, forming a triad of monuments with the cast-iron palmetto tree. This coordinated the building and monuments into a commemorative landscape that celebrated White South Carolinians' political dominance over the majority-Black population.

Wade Hampton Monument

Unveiled 1906

Frederick Wellington Ruckstull, sculptor

Like the Confederate Monument, the fifteen-foot-tall bronze equestrian sculpture of Wade Hampton III (1818–1902) celebrates White

Detail of the Wade Hampton Monument, showing Ruckstull's choice
to depict Hampton's head as he looked in the 1870s (as governor)
and his body in the 1860s (as Confederate general).
Photograph by Chandler Yonkers, 2020.

South Carolinians' pride in both the Confederacy and post-Reconstruction "redemption." Indeed, while the figure's head depicts Hampton as he appeared as a governor and US senator in the 1870s and 1880s, his uniformed body and mount convey him as a Confederate general. As a member of the state's richest antebellum planter family, commander of the Confederate cavalry, and the state's first post-Reconstruction governor, Hampton was the obvious hero for the state's elite at the beginning of the twentieth century. They widely credited him with honoring the Confederate cause, fighting for the rights of slaveholders, and wresting political power away from the federal government and newly enfranchised Black citizens after Reconstruction.[43]

Calls for a statue of Hampton began immediately after his 1902 death, and the state followed the next year with a $20,000 appropriation for an equestrian sculpture to be released once $10,000 had

Wade Hampton Monument. Photograph by Chandler Yonkers, 2020.

been raised by private subscription.[44] Competition with other Civil War monuments across the state and tensions between the United Daughters of the Confederacy (UDC) and other groups raising funds for the sculpture caused private donations to lag. The state ultimately made the appropriation despite the dearth of private donations.[45] A senator summarized the argument for the funding in a speech in the State House:

> While others failed, and the cause in which they fought ultimately was lost, his sword flashed only in the sunlight of success. . . . And when the war was over and his State was in the grasp of the conqueror, whose hatred could be appeased only by her degradation, and she was given over to pillage and sack by the vulgarest band of freebooters that ever preyed upon a prostrate State, and after eight long and humiliating years his people rose in their might and resolved to throw off the loathsome domination, and looked for a leader worthy of the great work they were about to undertake, all eyes with one accord turned to him, and

in one of the greatest civil revolutions that ever shed luster on the Anglo-Saxon race they prevailed.[46]

Inspired by the statue of Robert E. Lee on Richmond's Monument Avenue, a commission chose prominent artist Frederick Wellington Ruckstull to sculpt Hampton on a horse.[47] The artist represented Hampton "cantering down in front of the lines of his troops at review and saluting them as they cheered him"—a pose very similar to the statue of Union general John Frederick Hartranft that Ruckstull had recently completed for the Pennsylvania state capitol.[48] Ruckstull used a photograph of Hampton taken just after the 1876 gubernatorial election and the general's favorite sword to craft a model in his Paris studio.[49] Hampton's last paternalistic words— "My people, white and black—God bless them all"—were considered for the base's inscription, but ultimately the statue's base was inscribed with a list of his military and political positions and the Civil War battles in which he commanded.[50]

The commission and Ruckstull took the location and positioning of the statue seriously: this would be the largest piece of public art in the city, the first equestrian statue in the state, and the definitive representation of a widely beloved figure. A great believer in City Beautiful ideals, Ruckstull saw the statue as a catalyst for a coordinated improvement of the city's aesthetics. He suggested making Main Street an avenue of monuments and locating the Hampton statue in front of the federal building (now Columbia City Hall) facing south to the Confederate Monument and State House.[51] The state opted instead for a location on the east side of the State House grounds, across from Hampton's tomb at Trinity Cathedral. Ruckstull turned the statue to face west to suggest "the day when Gen. Hampton sadly withdrew his decimated command from the capital city and Sherman's army came into the city from the west."[52]

Hampton's granddaughters unveiled the statue on November 20, 1906, with some ten thousand people in attendance.[53] Most speeches and newspaper articles covering the unveiling praised Hampton explicitly for redeeming the state. The *Anderson Intelligencer,* for example, said, "He made it a State for white men and there is nothing

The Hampton Monument and George Washington statue in their original locations with Trinity Cathedral in the background, ca. 1909. Note the fountain and haphazard dirt paths. Courtesy of Richland Library, Columbia, S.C.

that white men should not do to honor him." Reports repeatedly demonized the African American and White Republican "carpet-baggers" expelled from the legislature in Hampton's 1876 election: "[The statue] that is to be unveiled today under the shadow of the capitol which he redeemed for us and purged of the vermin that had infested it will carry our story of affection down to many other generations who must learn from history and from it to love him as the people of this generation did."[54]

As Ruckstull predicted, the Hampton statue immediately inspired other monuments (including his commissions for the Partisan Generals and Confederate Women's Monuments) and calls for the general improvement of the State House grounds. But over time, the statue's base suffered from vandalism and lack of maintenance; many of the original metal letters on the base were missing, stolen, or broken by the late 1920s.[55] In consultation with Ruckstull in 1931, state historian Alexander Salley removed the letters and hired the

Columbia Stone Company to chisel them into the French granite.[56] The statue was moved to its current location in front of the Wade Hampton State Office Building and turned north to face the State House in the fall of 1969 as part of the redesign of the grounds.[57]

Partisan Generals Monument

Unveiled 1913

Frederick Wellington Ruckstull, sculptor

While he was working on the Wade Hampton Monument, Frederick Wellington Ruckstull completed the state's Revolutionary War monument commissioned by members of the South Carolina State Society of the Daughters of the American Revolution (DAR). It specifically recognizes commanders Thomas Sumter, Francis Marion, and Andrew Pickens but also the men who served under them. Each led their militias to decisive victories against the British in the state's swampy backcountry, earning Francis Marion the moniker "Swamp Fox" and Pickens and Sumter seats in the state legislature and US Congress after the war.[58] The DAR—including descendants of these three militia leaders—located the twenty-seven-foot-tall monument on the eastern edge of the grounds between Wade Hampton's grave and his equestrian monument. Although no longer extant (thanks to the relocation of the Hampton Monument in 1969), this invisible axis connected the state's Revolutionary, Civil War, and post-Reconstruction histories.

After a South Carolina senator's bill for a Francis Marion monument failed in the US Senate in the 1890s, the South Carolina DAR shifted the campaign to the state and expanded it to include three "partisan" generals (meaning they supported the patriot cause).[59] To prove that South Carolina was the "brightest gem in 'Liberty's Crown,'" DAR members Annie Robertson, Sara Richardson, and Rebecca Bacon raised $5,000 for the work and convinced the state

Partisan Generals Monument. Photograph by Chandler Yonkers, 2020.

to donate the site and an additional $2,000.[60] Their effort echoed White women's campaign for the Confederate Monument decades earlier and was the first in a long line of women's interventions and beautification efforts on the State House grounds in the twentieth century.

The DAR initially planned for the monument to make use of one of the columns damaged when contractors attempted to install it on the State House.[61] But plans changed when Robertson, an accomplished artist in her own right, engaged Ruckstull in 1904–5. While visiting Columbia to consult on the Wade Hampton Monument (and later on the Confederate Women's Monument), Ruckstull convinced Robertson and her compatriots "that a monument to victorious generals could not be a success begun with a broken column" and proposed a new design.[62] Following the ancient custom of using broken columns to memorialize lives cut short, the legislature agreed that the shaft would be "most eminently fitted for a symbol of the 'Lost Cause'" and allowed the women to use proceeds from its sale for Ruckstull's new design. The First Presbyterian Church purchased and dedicated the column as a monument to its congregation's Confederate veterans in its churchyard on Marion Street in 1920.[63]

Ruckstull's design for the Revolutionary War monument took more time and money than the women had initially imagined, but they had raised enough funds to engage the Davis Granite Company to carve a new column using polished pink granite by 1913.[64] Ruckstull chose the severe Doric order "to symbolize the Roman character and courage of those heroic generals and their soldiers who worked without pay for the love of cause and country." Holding a "palm of glory" and a "wreath of immortality," the winged victory atop the column is very similar to that on Ruckstull's Soldiers' and Sailors' Monument in New York City (dedicated in 1896 to Union soldiers). Ruckstull cast the bronze figure of victory, the railings around the base, and the portraits of the three commanders for the monument's base in his Paris studio.[65]

The monument's supporters used the Revolutionary generals' actions to legitimize those of South Carolina's more recent leaders. Like many of the period, the DAR believed that monuments offered tangible connections between past and present that could teach "patriotism and devotion to principle . . . unconsciously perhaps, but none the less surely in each oncoming generation"—thus "inculcating" the same values from the Revolution, through the Civil War and Reconstruction, to the present day.[66] The group chose the site on the east side of the State House grounds because it was located on an axis formed by Hampton's tomb at Trinity Cathedral and Ruckstull's recently completed equestrian statue of the general. Also active in the United Daughters of the Confederacy, these women framed Sumter, Marion, and Pickens as the direct predecessors of Confederate leaders like Wade Hampton, who defended their way of life against the US Army half a century after the Revolution.[67] At the monument's 1913 dedication, University of South Carolina history professor Yates Snowden described the partisan generals' achievements in terms remarkably similar to those used to describe Hampton's "redemption" that ended Reconstruction: "Driven from their gloomy and almost impenetrable swamps, even there the spirit of liberty survived, and South Carolina sustained by the examples of her Sumters and her Marions proved by her conduct that though her soil might be overrun, the spirit of her people was invincible!"[68]

Monument to the Women of the Confederacy (Confederate Women's Monument)

Unveiled 1912
Frederick Wellington Ruckstull, sculptor

The Monument to the South Carolina Women of the Confederacy commemorates White men's vision of White women's contributions to South Carolina during the Civil War. While at work on the monuments to Wade Hampton and the partisan generals in the first decade of the twentieth century, Frederick Wellington Ruckstull composed a work that combined "idealism and realism": accompanied by two angelic cherubs, the allegorical Genius of State crowns a "woman of the [eighteen] sixties" with victory.[69] As events proved, however, some White South Carolina women loathed to see their hard work

Monument to Confederate Women. Photograph by Chandler Yonkers, 2020.

reduced to a passive ideal despite the fact that it was rooted in the same Lost Cause ideology that they supported.

The United Confederate Veterans (UCV), an all-male group, initiated a campaign for monuments across the South to the women of the Confederacy at the end of the 1890s. It sought the endorsement and assistance of the leading Lost Cause women's organization, the United Daughters of the Confederacy, but the women refused to participate. They preferred that attention and resources go toward activities that would help the survivors of the war and their descendants more directly, including veterans' homes and educational campaigns. The women were also leery of competition with their own commemorative efforts, which had already resulted in monuments such as those to the partisan generals, Confederate dead, and Wade Hampton on the State House grounds. Most importantly, women rejected their husbands', fathers', and brothers' impulse to put them on pedestals—both literally and figuratively. The UCV's proposed monuments variously threatened to idealize them into unreachable and passive paragons, to patronize their past achievements, and to deny their present advocacy.[70] At least in part because of the UDC's opposition, the UCV's national movement fell apart and individual states began to take up the mantle.[71]

South Carolina first ratified a bill for "the erection of a monument to the women of the Confederacy on the state house grounds" in 1900 and the state was the first of seven southern states to build such a monument.[72] An aggressive media campaign led by the editor of the *State* newspaper raised more than half of the money for the monument, hired Ruckstull to design it, and worked closely with the legislature to help pay for the commission. The newspaper described the women to be honored as passive subjects in its initial fundraising plea: "The women of the Confederacy endured the privations and hardships of war, without its sustaining excitements. They waited and worked; their's [*sic*] was the torture of suspense."[73]

Ruckstull's resulting statue did indeed depict a passive model for women: as described by the artist, the figure looks "out into space with a firm, serene and courageous look, meditating over the past and the future" rather than actively at work nursing, mothering, or petitioning.[74] Sitting on a throne with the Bible open in her lap, she offers an unimpeachably pure example. The long inscription credits the "men of their state" for the monument, justifies the "righteous cause" of the Confederacy, and speaks to the "resurrection of truth with glorious vindication" that followed the end of Reconstruction. The winged figures confirm traditional gender roles: while the boy walks forward confidently, the girl shyly shrinks. Despite the national UDC's opposition to such monuments, the local chapter accepted the monument at its 1912 dedication, proclaiming "loyalty and consecration to the memories represented by this splendid gift."[75]

At Ruckstull's suggestion, the monument's commission placed the statue facing Senate Street at the end of the building's south steps

The Monument to Confederate Women at the bottom of the
State House's south steps at its 1912 unveiling. Courtesy of South
Caroliniana Library, University of South Carolina, Columbia, S.C.

on the opposite side of the Monument to the Confederate Dead. The
sculptor argued that "the women's monument has for its background
one of the finest porticos in the world" and encouraged the state to
finish the south side of the grounds to complete the setting.[76] He
surely envisioned Senate Street as a tree-lined avenue like that projected in Kelsey's master plan, but only a "beautiful bronze railing"
was placed around the work in the twentieth century. The railing was
hit by a car in 1927, and the UDC petitioned to move the statue away
from the street's "heavy traffic and turmoil."[77] Likely at the suggestion of the women, the monument was moved and tucked away in
the northeast corner of the grounds (where the Byrnes statue now
stands) in 1935. The state relocated it to its current position on the
southern edge of the Capitol Complex circa 1972. This step returned
the sculpture to its original axis and took the place of a fountain that
had been included in the modern master plan but scrapped because
of budgetary concerns.[78]

Spanish-American War Monuments

Installed on the State House grounds, 1913–41

Although the state of South Carolina sent fewer than one thousand soldiers to the Spanish-American War, that conflict is second only to the Civil War as the most-memorialized war on the State House grounds. Three monuments to that war were erected between 1900 and 1942: a cannon captured at Santiago, Cuba (scrapped in World War II, to leave behind only a granite base); a gun from the USS *Maine*; and a figural statue of an idealized soldier.

The United States intervened in Cuba's War of Independence from Spain after the explosion of the USS *Maine* in Havana Harbor on February 15, 1898. The ten-week conflict between the United States and Spain ended with 385 American combat casualties and Cuba's independence. Signed that December, the Treaty of Paris also made the United States an imperial power by conveying ownership of Spain's territories of Puerto Rico, Guam, and the Philippine Islands. Less than a quarter of South Carolina's National Guard was mobilized for the Spanish-American War. The state's poorly organized and equipped militia system delayed its participation while disease and poor nutrition rendered almost 39 percent of volunteers unfit for enlistment. The state's two regiments of racially segregated companies were mustered late in the conflict, and one regiment was not marshaled until August 1898, after the end of combat.[79]

Like other Spanish-American War monuments across the South, South Carolina's have more to do with the Civil War than the conflict with Spain. The Spanish-American War was the first military action in which southerners and northerners fought together since before the Civil War. Many White soldiers were the sons of Confederate veterans seeking the glories of their fathers. In popular literature and in speeches dedicating Spanish-American War monuments throughout the South—including those on the State House grounds—the reunification of White people in the North and South was praised as one of the most positive outcomes of the war.[80]

Mount for Spanish Cannon

The city of Columbia received its first "monument" to the Spanish-American War in 1900. The US government supplied a fourteen-foot-long brass muzzleloader captured by American forces during the Battle of Santiago, Cuba, in July 1898. Decorated with a Spanish inscription, the gun was made in Seville in November 1793.[81] Columbia was not the only American city to obtain such a relic of the Spanish-American War. Similar guns appeared in public parks throughout the country at the turn of the century.[82]

Despite city leaders' enthusiasm to decorate the grounds of the soon-to-be-completed State House with the cannon, the Spanish gun laid prostrate on the construction site for close to a year until Columbia's city council promised to mount it properly. The original location proposed was "in front of the Confederate monument,

Columbia High School's "most attractive boy and girl" of 1929—Nancy Phillips and Tommy Scott—pose in costumes next to the Spanish cannon in *The Columbian* yearbook.

Mount for Spanish Cannon. Photograph by Chandler Yonkers, 2020.

aiming up main street," but the gun was ultimately mounted in 1900 on a square granite carriage on the west side of the State House.[83] It was a regular stop for citizens exploring the grounds and a delight for climbing children.[84]

In the fall of 1942 the state gathered a collection of scrap metal from the State House grounds that included the Spanish cannon, a handful of Civil War cannons and World War I guns, defunct cast-iron pipes, and a bell that had once hung in Columbia's City Hall as part of a national effort to help support the effort for World War II. The public largely regarded such recycling as a more useful fate for the cannon than decorating the State House grounds. The *Columbia Record* estimated that the Spanish gun could be transformed into "500,000 thirty caliber cartridges, or untold numbers of 50 caliber cartridges, 20 mm anti-aircraft cannon shells, 37 mm shells, or even several hundred 75 mm shells."[85] The *State's* editor even heralded the removal of such "war souvenirs . . . of dubious decorative utility" as an opportunity to clean up the cluttered memorial landscape.[86] Whatever the actual impact on weapon production, such recycling efforts rallied patriotism and encouraged thrift on the home front.[87] Today the cannon's original granite mount sits near its original location with two plaques: one commemorates the original cannon while the other recognizes the civilian effort for World War II.

Gun from the USS *Maine*. Photograph by Chandler Yonkers, 2020.

Gun from the USS *Maine*

The city of Columbia successfully applied to the US government for a relic from the USS *Maine* following the dramatic and highly publicized raising of the battleship from the Havana Harbor in 1910. A 2.5-inch, six-pounder gun arrived in Columbia in July 1913, and the city council installed the relic in Irwin Park as "a lasting ornament to the pretty park."[88] At the western end of the city's electric streetcar line along the Columbia Canal, Irwin Park already featured a zoo, sculptures, elaborate plantings, and the city's water treatment plant.[89]

After the expansion of the city's water treatment plant shuttered the park in the 1910s, the state's Spanish-American War veterans called for the gun's transfer to the State House grounds.[90] The legislature agreed that "many people had lost sight of the fact that the gun was in Columbia" and authorized local Masons to construct a concrete base for the gun across from the US post office (now the home of the supreme court) on Gervais Street in 1931.[91]

The city of Columbia presented the gun to the Spanish War Veterans of Columbia during their annual reunion and the state's fair

Spanish War Veterans Monument. Photograph by Chandler Yonkers, 2020

week that October.[92] With a Confederate battle flag draping the gun (along with a Union Jack and a US flag), speakers heralded the war as a moment of reconciliation between North and South. One praised the veterans present for "heal[ing] the breach brought about by the Confederate war," while another recognized that the conflict had come "after 33 years of peace, peace after the heart rending contest between brothers in the North and in the South."[93]

Spanish War Veterans Monument
Theo Alice Ruggles Kitson, sculptor

While the Spanish cannon mount and the gun from the USS *Maine* commemorate America's victory in the Spanish-American War, the statue on the east side of the State House's north axis specifically recognizes the sacrifices of South Carolina's few veterans of the conflict. Organizing for a memorial began in 1936 among the members of the David DuBose Gaillard Camp and its women's auxiliary.[94] The statewide South Carolina Spanish War veterans organization formed a memorial committee later that year, claiming "that the

Spanish-American war had been ended for nearly a half century and that not a single memorial monument or tablet to the veterans had been erected in the state."[95]

By 1941 the veterans had raised $1,500, secured $1,550 from the state legislature, and obtained $750 from the city of Columbia.[96] The monument was unveiled that fall with veterans and politicians in attendance. They echoed the sentiments of earlier Spanish-American War monument dedications. Governor and senator-elect Burnet Rhett Maybank recalled the American Revolution in his speech about the Cubans' struggle for independence: "It is a monument to those who fought to establish the right of a free people to govern themselves; with a free press, freedom of religion and freedom of the seas."[97]

Initial plans were to erect the monument near the Spanish cannon on the grounds' west side.[98] The memorial's ultimate location was instead directly across from the sculpture of Benjamin Ryan Tillman, erected the previous year. Over the course of planning the monument, the veterans evidently changed its site to complement Tillman's. The finished sculpture clearly imitates that of Tillman: both are nine-foot-high, one and one-half times life size, bronze, figural statues on matching stepped granite bases.[99]

The bronze soldier atop the granite base of South Carolina's Spanish War Veterans Monument wears a uniform fit for combat in a tropical locale: his open collar, rolled sleeves, baggy pants, and high leather boots form a uniform far more casual than those of earlier conflicts. His hands grip a gun at his waist, while his steady gaze looks to the horizon beneath a broad-brimmed hat. Known as the *Hiker,* this statue is a cast of a work by Theo Alice Ruggles Kitson. The first woman elected to the National Sculpture Society, Kitson originally sculpted the *Hiker* to commemorate Spanish-American War veterans at the University of Minnesota in 1906. Gorham Manufacturing Company obtained the rights to the statue in 1921 and began to mass-produce it.[100] Casts of Kitson's *Hiker* may now be found in public parks across the country. It is the only monument by a female sculptor on the SC State House grounds.

The choice of an idealized White soldier for the monument denies the participation of African American servicemen in the

Spanish-American War. As a mass-produced image found in public spaces nationwide, it also confirms the narrative of many White Americans of the early twentieth century that the Spanish-American War finally succeeded in uniting White men of the North and South.[101]

James Marion Sims Monument

Unveiled 1929
Edward Thomas Quinn, sculptor
Harold Sterner and Lafaye and Lafaye, architects

South Carolina physicians began to discuss a monument to pioneering gynecologist James Marion Sims (1813–83) for the State House grounds shortly after the unveiling of the Wade Hampton Monument in 1906.[102] They lamented the fact that New York City had recognized Sims with a life-size statue in 1894 but that he remained largely unknown in his home state.[103] A group of their wives, the Women's Auxiliary of the South Carolina Medical Association, ultimately ensured that Sims was the second South Carolinian to be commemorated with his own memorial on the grounds two decades later.

Born in Lancaster and educated at the University of South Carolina (then South Carolina College), Sims began his career in South Carolina and Alabama in the 1840s just as the medical field was professionalizing and before the invention of modern anesthesia. He gained international fame after devising a surgical method for treating vesico-vaginal fistula (a condition in which an opening develops between the bladder and vagina) by operating on enslaved African American women. A slaveowner himself, Sims used prevailing notions of their biological inferiority to support the experimental surgeries, including claims that Black women could not experience pain or immodesty as White women might. Sims had unlimited and unquestioned power over their bodies, even if these women may

Detail of the Sims Monument. Photograph by Chandler Yonkers, 2020.

have benefited from his surgeries.[104] Sims continued to develop new gynecological methods and instruments in New York and Europe before becoming president of the American Medical Association and the American Gynecological Society at the end of his life.[105]

Aided by Lancaster politicians, the South Carolina Medical Association began a campaign in earnest for a monument to Sims in 1910.[106] They secured a $5,000 appropriation from the legislature in 1912 and sought to raise additional funds for a statue of "heroic size" that could compete with New York City's.[107] Recognizing the fund-raising achievements of the women around them as well as Sims's gynecological specialization, they hoped that "the women's clubs in particular should be invited to take a hand in the matter. For it was among the women that the noble physician did his greatest work."[108]

The association's campaign failed, leaving its women's auxiliary to revive the campaign along the same lines more than a decade later. Led by Daisy Lee Stuckey of Sumter and formed in 1923, the South Carolina Women's Auxiliary was one of many groups of White physicians' wives encouraged in the period by the American Medical Association. The Sims monument was the auxiliary's first major project.[109]

Facing difficulties fundraising for a life-size statue, the auxiliary ultimately settled on a more modest and architectural monument for "our greatest benefactor" with a total budget of $6,256 (including the original state appropriation).[110] It hired New York architect Harold Sterner and local firm Lafaye and Lafaye to design a stepped, shrine-like granite setting. Edward Thomas Quinn, a New York artist with a number of monument commissions nationwide, used photographs of Sims to design the bronze bust for the composition's central niche.[111] The auxiliary erected the monument facing toward the University of South Carolina on the southeast corner of Senate and Sumter Streets in 1929 to inspire passing students.[112] Carolina students instead vandalized the monument multiple times over the following decades, often painting the bust red after sports victories over rival Clemson University.[113] The monument was moved to its current location and turned to face the capitol in 1969 as part of Robert Marvin's redesign of the grounds.[114]

1930 advertisement for the Consolidated Granite Company featuring the Sims Monument in its original location. Materials and labor for these monuments were often donated in return for such publicity. Courtesy of Richland Library, Columbia, S.C.

The campaigns for the New York and South Carolina sculptures—as well as the South Carolina monument's inscription—praised Sims for his treatment of both "empress and slave."[115] Admiration for his supposed magnanimity has recently soured as historians and activists recognize his medical experiments' systemic dehumanization of enslaved women. New York City removed its sculpture of Sims in the spring of 2018, arguing that the monument had "come to represent a legacy of oppressive and abusive practices on bodies that were seen as subjugated, subordinate, and exploitable in service to his fame."[116]

Jefferson Davis and Robert E. Lee Memorial Highway Markers

Unveiled 1923 and 1938

As part of national movements to name interstate highways after Confederate general Robert E. Lee (1807–70) and president Jefferson Davis (1808–89) in the early twentieth century, the state division of the United Daughters of the Confederacy dedicated two routes through South Carolina to these men. Designated in 1923, the Jefferson Davis Memorial Highway crossed South Carolina from its southwest corner to its northeast (now US-1). Recognized in 1938, the Robert E. Lee Memorial Highway stretched across the state from its southeast to northwest corners (in a route later consumed by I-26). Both highways met in Columbia and were marked with granite boulders now located along the northern perimeter of the State House grounds.

Founded at the State House in May 1896, the South Carolina branch of the UDC's mission was to connect past to present. The organization's monuments and public celebrations justified and legitimized slavery, the Confederacy, and Jim Crow.[117] Jefferson Davis and

Robert E. Lee were particular heroes for the White-women-only organization: while its members praised Lee for his character in the face of defeat, they martyred Davis for his suffering after the war.[118]

Jefferson Davis Memorial Highway Marker

The national UDC began its "most stupendous undertaking" in 1913: organizing state chapters to dedicate and beautify existing highways in memory of Jefferson Davis. Begun at a time when state transportation departments were weak or nonexistent and the interstate highway system was just beginning to formalize, its members hoped to use the designation to tell "one of the most wonderful stories of history and of the South, and devotion to a great cause; the story that will link the days of long ago with descendant dreams and faith in a great future, the recompense of loyalty to an ideal."[119] The effort was a challenge to the formation of the coast-to-coast Lincoln Highway that stretched 4,600 continuous miles by 1941.[120] When the 4,339 members of the UDC's South Carolina division dedicated the Jefferson Davis Memorial Highway in 1923, the highway consisted of

Jefferson Davis Memorial Highway Marker.
Photograph by Chandler Yonkers, 2020.

Route 50 from Cheraw to Columbia and Route 12 from Columbia to North Augusta.[121]

The UDC initially installed the granite boulder that currently sits on the State House grounds on the 1600 block of Taylor Street (behind the Robert Mills House). The November 1923 festivities included a parade, pageant, and an unveiling by the young descendants of Jefferson Davis and Robert E. Lee—a common strategy at such ceremonies to symbolize the passing of "Confederate" values across generations.[122] Made of donated local granite, the marker matched the standard form and inscription of those used to identify the highway in other states and was very similar to the marker for the old State House that would be erected in 1938.[123] Speakers at the dedication praised the boulder for its "solidity, its dignity, its stability, uprightness, its power of resistance and endurance and spoke of the tragedy of the life of the one president of the Confederacy. . . . South Carolina is loyal to the Stars and Stripes and is ready with her sons and daughters to serve our flag, yet reverently and forever will she preserve the memory of the leader of the Lost Cause."[124]

Although one member promised at the dedication that the boulder would "not budge an inch unless a Japanese earthquake takes a notion to emigrate to the United States of America," the Davis highway marker was moved when the South Carolina Highway Department diverted US-1 from Taylor Street to the newly widened Gervais Street in 1949.[125] This was a common outcome for the Jefferson Davis Memorial Highway across the country: as highways transitioned from a loose group of private, local, or state roads into a highly regulated federal system (especially after major legislation in 1921 and 1953), many memorial markers were moved, roads renamed, and designations forgotten.[126] The Columbia marker was moved to its current location within the confines of the grounds in 1962 after Gervais Street was widened again.[127]

Robert E. Lee Memorial Highway Marker

The UDC's efforts to dedicate a system of interstate highways to Robert E. Lee were not as successful as those for the Jefferson Davis Memorial Highway. By 1938 the Robert E. Lee Memorial Highway extended through North and South Carolina to connect to Virginia and Tennessee.[128] The South Carolina legislature dedicated the "route from Charleston by way of Columbia to Greenville" to Lee and authorized the UDC to erect markers in 1938.[129] Most of the roads along the route were supplanted by the construction of I-26 from 1957 through 1969, leaving behind the marker on the State House grounds.[130]

Detail of the Confederate seal on the Robert E. Lee Memorial Highway Marker. Photograph by Chandler Yonkers, 2020.

CONFEDERATE FLAG FORMED BY 1000 SCHOOL CHILDREN ON STEPS OF STATE HOUSE, COLUMBIA, S. C.

One thousand people form a "living Confederate flag" at the dedication of the Robert E. Lee Memorial Highway, 1938. Historic Columbia Collection, HCF 2018.6.26

Bearing a bronze depiction of the seal of the Confederate States of America and engraved with the names of the UDC members who led the campaign, the granite boulder marking the Robert E. Lee Memorial Highway was dedicated on the State House grounds as part of the 1938 national reunion of Confederate veterans.[131] The UDC explicitly connected their dead heroes with living generations at the ceremony: more than one thousand Columbians dressed in red, white, and blue created a "living Confederate flag" on the state-house steps.[132] The president of the UDC, Dorothy Lamar, spoke of the value of Lee's example of "pure Americanism" as threats of communism loomed.[133]

Memorial Trees on the State House Grounds

A number of trees have been planted around the capitol in memory of individuals or groups of people. Because of the haphazard maintenance of the State House grounds and the ephemeral nature of such "living memorials," most of the trees (and the markers that accompanied them) either do not survive or are now impossible to identify.

Americans have planted trees or dedicated living trees to commemorate individuals since the Revolutionary period. As growing, organic things, these markers connect the past and present in ways that are potentially more evocative than static or representational monuments made of stone or metal.[134] On the State House grounds and in many other public spaces in America, memorial trees related to George Washington are especially prevalent. The propagation of clippings from trees important to Washington's biography reached the height of popularity during the 1932 bicentennial of his birth, a national celebration that resulted in 4.7 million local commemorations.[135]

Marker for a tree dedicated to Robert E. Lee (the tree does not survive). Photograph by Chandler Yonkers, 2020.

At least two such trees survive today. The South Carolina chapter of the Daughters of the American Revolution planted the first, a seedling descended from the Cambridge, Massachusetts, elm under which Washington took command of the Continental Army, as part of the city's celebration of the Washington Bicentennial in 1932.[136] The group installed a granite and bronze marker at the clipping's base after "an elaborate patriotic parade down Main Street" that included boy scouts, the National Guard, war veterans, local and state officials, and DAR members from across the country.[137] The tree was replaced in 1975 and then again with the current sawtooth oak and marker in 1988.

The South Carolina DAR planted the second in the vicinity of the Cambridge elm descendant with another clipping in the years following World War II.[138] The women imagined a "State Tribute Grove" of trees around the Tillman statue as a statement of American values in the face of communism. A speaker pronounced at the dedication: "Symbols such as this tree . . . must be remembered and utilized as bulwarks against the insidious attacks of foreign ideologies."[139] Although this tree and its plaque survive, it is unclear how many others in its vicinity were originally part of the tribute grove.

Other memorial trees have been planted on the grounds over the years:

- In 1905 the DAR planted an Osage orange clipping from the site of its national headquarters, Continental Hall in Washington,

DC, on the east side of the State House grounds (where the DAR later erected the Partisan Generals Monument).[140] It no longer survives.

➤ The UDC planted two trees on the State House grounds in memory of Robert E. Lee, but the plaque for only one survives. The Wade Hampton chapter planted a dogwood tree and installed a plaque in 1935; it had wandered to another tree by 1962 (it now sits on the east side of the grounds near the African American History Monument).[141] The South Carolina Division planted another to mark the dedication of the Robert E. Lee Memorial Highway in 1938.[142]

➤ A tree "dedicated to the children of South Carolina" was planted as part of the South Carolina Congress of Parents and Teachers in 1930.[143] It is not clear if there ever was a plaque installed or where the tree was located.

➤ The Ann Pamela Cunningham chapter of the DAR planted a seedling grown from a walnut tree standing at Washington's Mount Vernon plantation in Virginia as part of the organization's celebrations of the bicentennial of the first president's birth. They planted it with trowels made from wood and metal salvaged from Cunningham's family plantation in Laurens County (she was the founder of the Mount Vernon Ladies' Association of the Union, which preserved Washington's home).[144] If the tree survives, it is unidentified today.

➤ In 1943 the Crown Cork & Seal Company planted two cork oak seedlings on the grounds (accompanied by a plaque) to "promote the cultivation of cork trees in the state" just east of the Partisan Generals Monument.[145]

➤ A seedling from an oak in Independence Square, Philadelphia, was supposedly planted in 1951 to mark the 150th anniversary of the Declaration of Independence, but it was unidentifiable by 1967.[146]

John C. Calhoun State Office Building.
Photograph by Chandler Yonkers, 2020.

John C. Calhoun
State Office Building

Built 1925–6
Harold Tatum and Milton Medary Jr., architects

The John C. Calhoun State Office Building was the first answer to the state's desperate, long-deferred need for office space. Built on Senate Street (closed to traffic in 1969), the building's limestone facing and Renaissance Revival style complemented the State House from a deferential distance.[147] It was known simply as the "state office building" until 1940, when it was renamed for nineteenth-century congressman, secretary of war, US vice president, and US senator from South Carolina, John C. Calhoun (1782–1850), to avoid being confused with the Wade Hampton State Office Building.[148]

The first legislature and supreme court to occupy the State House in 1869 found its square footage inadequate almost immediately. Calls to build a stand-alone office building grew louder following the completion of the building's dome in 1903.[149] Over the next decade legislators weighed concerns over the potential cost of a new building, the portion of the state budget spent leasing office space, and the expense of inefficiencies caused by spreading state employees throughout downtown Columbia. By 1922, for example, the state was spending more than $18,000 each year to rent 14,801 square feet in buildings such as the Union National Bank Building (located at 1200 Main Street directly across from the State House).[150] With the argument that "such a structure would result in a substantial saving to the state," the General Assembly finally borrowed $400,000 from

SOUTH CAROLINA STATE OFFICE BUILDING. COLUMBIA. S. C.

The State Office Building in a 1937 postcard. Note the top two stories, which the legislature initially rejected but later decided to build as designed. This space includes a courtroom planned for the state's supreme court that remained unused until the 1980s.
Courtesy of Richland Library, Columbia, S.C.

the sinking fund to construct an office building in early 1924.[151] It hired Harold Tatum, a young architect trained in the Beaux-Arts tradition at the University of Pennsylvania and working locally, who associated nationally renowned architect Milton Medary Jr. on the project.[152]

In November 1924 the architects proposed a dignified design that could be built in "two bites": a five-story, limestone-covered steel structure crowned by a two-story brick-faced pavilion.[153] Although the newspaper graciously claimed that the arrangement "reliev[ed] the monotony which would have marred the beauty of the structure had it been entirely of the limestone," the design pragmatically anticipated the subsequent battle over costs and square footage.[154] The state initially approved $500,000 for the six-story structure, but rising construction costs and the fickle demands of its potential tenants—the supreme court and state's Highway Department— stalled the project, threatened to kill it in the legislature, and resulted in the removal of the two-story brick pavilion from the design to reduce costs by the time construction began in June 1925.[155] The legislature relented halfway through the construction the next year, ultimately deciding to fund the construction of the top two floors according to Tatum's and Medary's original plans after all.[156]

Even though the top floor was originally designed with a courtroom and library for the South Carolina Supreme Court, the court found the space inadequate, never moved in, and remained in the State House until it renovated the former post office on Gervais Street for its use in 1971.[157] The ornate barrel-vaulted courtroom was converted into office space and forgotten behind a drop ceiling until it was renovated for the state's court of appeals in the 1980s.[158]

Wade Hampton State Office Building (with statue in front).
Photograph by Chandler Yonkers, 2020.

Wade Hampton
State Office Building

Built 1938–40
Lafaye, Lafaye and Fair with Hopkins and Baker, architects

The Wade Hampton State Office Building is slightly bigger and plainer than its neighbor to the east, although its limestone exterior, recessed top story, and position along the former Senate Street complements the John C. Calhoun State Office Building and the State House. Together the two office buildings formed a core of state buildings anticipating the Capitol Complex that would incorporate them decades later.[159] Constructed under Franklin Delano Roosevelt's New Deal, the Wade Hampton Building's restrained Stripped

Classical exterior and elegantly simple Art Deco interiors are typical of structures funded by the Public Works Administration.

Within a decade of the dedication of the Calhoun Building, South Carolina had "entirely outgrown" its office space, and the legislature began discussing adding onto the State House, commissioning a new building, or purchasing one of the downtown skyscrapers it was already leasing.[160] The promise of a 45 percent match from the Public Works Administration for materials and labor costs encouraged legislators to decide on a new building and quieted the kinds of debates that had complicated the construction of the Calhoun Building. In a little more than a year, the state designated almost $500,000 from the sinking fund; purchased land west of the Calhoun Building; hired South Carolina architecture firms Lafaye, Lafaye and Fair and Hopkins and Baker; and constructed a building that "outwardly would harmonize in appearance with the existing state office building" with 25 percent more square footage.[161]

Built with separate bathrooms for African American citizens, as was typical of southern public buildings of the period, the building housed the State Department for Education throughout the state government's stalwart defense of racial segregation in public schools in the 1950s.[162] The statue of its namesake, Confederate general and post-Reconstruction governor Wade Hampton III, was relocated in front of the building in 1969.

Stars on the State House and Marker for the First State House

Installed 1928–38
Alexander Samuel Salley Jr., historian

Several markers from the 1930s explain the damage at the State House grounds that occurred when Union general William Tecumseh Sherman captured Columbia just short of the end of the Civil War. Much of the city and the State House grounds burned on February 17, 1865, thanks to Sherman's troops as well as strong winds and miscalculations made by Confederate general Wade Hampton (the leader memorialized by an equestrian statue on the east side of the grounds).[163] Alexander Samuel Salley Jr., the first head of the state's Historical Commission from 1905 until his retirement in 1949, called attention to the visible results of the siege in order to demonize the federal government for its supposed barbarism and to cast the Confederates in a positive light by contrast. A self-taught historian who advocated tirelessly for the preservation of the state's records in the face of perpetually paltry state funding, Salley was also a proponent of the Lost Cause.

As state historian, Salley collected and safeguarded South Carolina's important records in the State House until moving the archive to the War Memorial Building in 1935 (now on the University of South Carolina campus).[164] He also played a significant role in the memorial function of the State House grounds over the first half of the twentieth century. His research provided information for the various groups and legislators seeking to erect monuments. He tried to repair the broken cane on the statue of George Washington and maintained a relationship with Frederick Wellington Ruckstull, consulting the artist on the maintenance of his various sculptures.[165]

Between 1928 and 1938, Salley highlighted the damage done to the grounds during the 1865 siege with a plaque on the Washington statue's base, a marker for the first State House, and stars and explanations affixed to the State House's exterior. The efforts positioned South Carolina as a victim of the Civil War, echoing the arguments for sovereignty in Henry Kirke Brown's antebellum sculpture and the stories of "survival" in the grounds' many post-Reconstruction monuments.[166] Columbia's 1936 sesquicentennial, ongoing discussions about additions to the State House, nationwide Lost Cause sentiment, and Salley's own research on the history of the building motivated these interventions.[167]

A couple reads the plaques on the side of the State House, 1968.
Note the stars affixed to the side of the building. Courtesy of
Richland Library, Columbia, S.C.

Stars and Plaques on the Northwest Corner
of the State House

Rather than repair the damaged granite blocks of the State House's walls, the state has allowed the marred walls to remain a visible reminder of the Civil War. Walter E. Duncan, a state legislator and newspaperman from Aiken, suggested installing markers on the building's exterior in 1928.[168] Two brass Confederate cannons then stored in the basement were quickly melted to produce six bronze stars, which were affixed to the west side of the State House "each at a place where a 'yankee' bullet struck" and to bring "to the minds of the living a thought as to the manner of men who wore the gray and the sacrifices which they made in an effort to establish a Southern Confederacy."[169] Salley wrote explanatory text for two tablets in which he used the term "honorable scar," the same phrase employed to describe the amputations of Civil War veterans.[170] This likened the State House to a human body and testified to the emotions still attached to the event more than sixty years after the end of the war.

In 1936 Salley removed the two metal plaques and directed the engraving of four new inscriptions onto the granite blocks of the State House walls the next year.[171] Masons from the Columbia Stone Company ridged the surfaces of the stones and then smoothed them for carving.[172] The two inscriptions on the west side of the building revised the text from the plaques explaining the stars (this time forgoing the term "honorable scar"), while the two on the north portico's steps gave short histories of the building and cited John Rudolph Niernsee as the building's architect. As a believer that the building was "still in many respects incomplete" without Niernsee's tower, Salley's inscription was likely a jab at the legislature for failing to complete the State House as designed.[173]

Marker for the Old State House

In 1938 Salley again led the charge for the recognition of the Civil War's destruction when he oversaw the unveiling of a marker "near the western side of the State House to mark the location of the old

The Old State House Marker. Photograph by Chandler Yonkers, 2020.

capitol."[174] Despite the marker's tombstone-like shape and tone (the inscription reads "here stood the old state house"), the building it memorializes likely would have been demolished shortly after the war even if it had not burned in February 1865. The new State House under construction at the time of the fire would have made the old wooden building superfluous upon completion. The marker erroneously recognizes Irish immigrant James Hoban (the architect of the White House in Washington, DC) as the architect of the original State House, an attribution that has since been disproven. The marker was moved around 1969 to make way for the Palmetto Monument and new path system, so it no longer rests atop the site of the old State House.

Benjamin Ryan Tillman Monument

Unveiled 1940
Frederick C. Hibbard, sculptor

The monument to former South Carolina governor and US senator Benjamin Ryan Tillman (1847–1918) still stands in its original location, which was opposite the statue of his political adversary and predecessor, Wade Hampton, until it was moved in 1969. Politician Jimmy Byrnes (whose monument sits in the northeast corner of the grounds) gave the speech at the statue's unveiling, describing the grounds as a "battlefield" and Tillman as the leader who "walked through the valley [with the masses], and who understood their needs and who would fight unwaveringly for their cause."[175] Erected in the same years that civil rights gained traction in South Carolina, Tillman's steely, one-eyed gaze fixed directly on Hampton and suggested that the most violent and aggressive form of Jim Crow would prevail.

The Benjamin Ryan Tillman Monument, facing the
Spanish War Veterans Monument across the north axis of
the State House. Photograph by Chandler Yonkers, 2020.

Born to a slave-owning planter family in Edgefield, Tillman explicitly used White supremacy to build a political coalition of poor
White farmers devastated by the Civil War. He used violence, in-
timidation, and fraud to regain political power from the African
American Republicans who had led the state government during

Reconstruction. He then pushed back against fellow Democrats like Hampton who had been elected to overthrow the Republicans, criticizing them for elitism and courting Black voters. As governor from 1890 to 1894, "Pitchfork Ben" led the charge for a new state constitution, legislating the suppression of African Americans' voting rights. He also helped to establish Clemson and Winthrop Colleges for White South Carolinians while harboring life-long beliefs about the dangers of educating African Americans. Tillman brought his arguments to the US Senate from 1895 to 1918, where he advocated for funding for his home state and mentored a young Jimmy Byrnes.[176]

The erection of the monument to James Marion Sims in 1929 inspired governor John Gardiner Richards Jr. to campaign for a life-size statue of Tillman on the State House grounds.[177] As a longtime supporter and protégé of Tillman, Richards understood the statue as a commemoration of his own political legacy (his name appears on the back corner of the statue's base).[178] Although he formed a commission and the state appropriated $10,000 for the work in 1930, Richards's fundraising stalled during the Great Depression.[179]

In 1937 Richards resumed the monument effort in earnest and by 1939 had raised $6,000 to add to the state's contribution.[180] His commission chose Chicago sculptor Frederick C. Hibbard to design the one and one-half times life-size bronze sculpture and stepped granite base, favoring a pose in which Tillman stood "alone" without leaning on a support.[181] The final figure holds a rolled piece of paper (perhaps a reference to the 1895 South Carolina Constitution) and realistically depicts Tillman's missing left eye (lost after a childhood injury). Three thousand people came to see the sculpture unveiled on May 1, 1940, and heard Byrnes dub Tillman "the first New Dealer" for his defense of poor White farmers.[182]

By memorializing Tillman's earlier brand of violent voter suppression and racism, the monument reaffirmed the Jim Crow system in the early years of White South Carolinians' fight against integration. In both Richards's campaign and in a plaque on the final monument, supporters praised Tillman as an "outspoken defender of the rights of the common people."[183] Yet "common" meant *White,* and always at the expense of African Americans. In speeches and pamphlets, the

The Tillman Monument in 1949. Note the lack of paths, planting, and benches around it. Courtesy of Richland Library, Columbia, S.C.

monument's patrons explicitly praised Tillman's efforts for the 1895 constitution because it "legally disenfranchised the negroes" and gave the "common white man ... a firmer hold on political power."[184] This was an affront to the civil rights movement then gaining ground in the state as Black South Carolinians advocated for antilynching legislation, equal access to jobs under the New Deal, and their right to vote. Black activists such as Modjeska Simkins galvanized by organizing across the state, resulting in the South Carolina Conference of the NAACP in 1939 just months before the dedication of the Tillman statue.[185]

Replica of the Liberty Bell. Photograph by Chandler Yonkers, 2020.

Liberty Bell Replica

Unveiled 1950

This 20,080-pound replica of the Liberty Bell is one of fifty-four that the US Treasury Department distributed to each American state and territory as part of its marketing for Independence Savings Bonds in 1950.[186] Cast in 1751 for Pennsylvania's colonial capitol building in Philadelphia (later known as "Independence Hall"), the Liberty Bell is one of the most iconic American symbols.[187] Its famous crack was painted onto each of the mid-twentieth-century replicas.

The US government had used the Liberty Bell in its patriotic advertising campaigns to sell Liberty Bonds during both world wars before commissioning a French foundry to cast copies during the

Korean War in 1950.[188] Funded by various American metal companies and touring the country in specially designed Ford trucks, the bells encouraged Americans to buy savings bonds to fund and rally patriotism around the Cold War.[189] President Harry Truman declared the replicas as representations of American and democratic ideals in the face of "Communist imperialism—a reactionary movement that despises liberty and is the mortal foe of personal freedom."[190]

South Carolina's own "symbol of freedom" was installed on July 4, 1950, just to the east of the State House's north steps (opposite the Palmetto Monument in the spot formerly occupied by the Confederate and Washington Monuments).[191] Critics noted it was "simply a glossed up publicity stunt for the Liberty Savings Bond drive" and worried that the grounds were becoming too crowded with monuments.[192] The bell was moved to its current location in 1973 as part of the renovation of the State House grounds and has been rung numerous times to mark various patriotic anniversaries and celebrations.[193]

Confederate Battle Flag

On State House grounds, 1938–2015

A Confederate battle flag flew on a pole mounted just behind the Confederate Monument from 2000 until 2015, making South Carolina the last southern state to display that flag on its capitol grounds.[194] The first Confederate flag to hang in the capitol appeared in the House chamber in 1938 as a challenge to federal antilynching legislation, joined by another in the Senate to push back against federal mandates over racial integration in 1956.[195] The legislature first hung the Confederate flag on a pole affixed to the exterior of the building in 1961 and then atop the dome in 1962 (along with the state and US flags).[196] Legislators flew it to commemorate the centennial

of the Civil War as well as to push back against African Americans protesting segregation and other civil injustices on the State House grounds. The first African American legislators elected since Reconstruction began protesting the flag in the 1970s, prompting Whites to argue that the flag was a symbol of the state's proud history rather than racism.[197]

After decades of debate, public outcry, lawsuits, and finally economic boycotts of the state by the NAACP, the General Assembly passed legislation to remove the flag. Passed largely along racial lines, the legislation was a compromise between those who supported the flag and those who saw it as a symbol of oppression: it did not banish the flag entirely from the grounds but rather relocated it from atop to the dome to a new pole adjacent to the Confederate Monument. It also included a provision aimed to preempt any further debate on monuments at the State House grounds and beyond.[198] The Heritage Act of 2000 specified that no war or African American

The Confederate flag is removed from its final location next to the Confederate Monument, July 10, 2015. Photograph by Tim Dominick of the *State* newspaper.

history monuments on state property could be "relocated, removed, disturbed, or altered" and that no place named after a historic person or event in the state could be renamed without a two-thirds vote in each branch of the General Assembly.[199] By requiring such a majority on a highly controversial topic, the Heritage Act suppressed any future attempts to remove the flag or alter other monuments across South Carolina.

The General Assembly finally banished the flag from the State House grounds entirely in 2015 after a White supremacist murdered nine African Americans at Mother Emanuel AME Church in Charleston. Nikki Haley, the state's first female and first Indian American governor, explained the decision: "These grounds are a place that everybody should feel a part of. . . . There is a place for that flag. It's not in a place that represents all people in South Carolina."[200] The flag is now part of the collection of the SC Confederate Relic Room and Military Museum.

THREE

Building for Bureaucracy
(1969–present)

The 1970s witnessed the doubling of the land area of the State House grounds, the construction or renovation of tens of thousands of square feet of office and parking space, and the rearrangement of many of its monuments and axes. "Fertilized" by President Lyndon B. Johnson's Great Society, the number and outreach of South Carolina's governmental agencies had expanded greatly in the 1960s.[1] This growing bureaucracy finally confronted legislators' reluctance to spend money on office space and prompted long-needed improvements to the landscape. The scale of the state's changes to the State House grounds from 1969 to 1981 was larger and far more coordinated than any other in its 150-year history.

These tremendous physical changes accompanied massive shifts in who used the State House grounds and how they did so. Beginning in the late 1950s, White "redeemers" lost exclusive control over the grounds' meaning as African Americans advocated for their rights at the State House. Their protests challenged the narratives of racial hierarchy built into the landscape while their votes and advocacy began to change the makeup of the General Assembly. In 1970–71, James Felder, I. S. Leevy Johnson, and Herbert Fielding became the first African Americans since Reconstruction to sit as elected members of the legislature in the State House.

The changing General Assembly reimagined the site as a civic center that looked forward rather than backward. Local architecture firm Lyles, Bissett, Carlisle & Wolff designed a complex that respected the State House and Calhoun and Hampton Buildings with

The State House, ca. 1950. Note the parking lot around the Confederate Monument, the locations of the Liberty Bell and Palmetto Monuments, the flattened space around the building, and the system of paths, all of which would change by 1969–70. Courtesy of South Caroliniana Library, University of South Carolina, Columbia, S.C.

axial symmetry and limestone cladding but also boldly announced South Carolina's future with Brutalist architecture lacking classical column capitals or other historical trappings. The massive parking facility beneath them accommodated close to two thousand employees using the latest advances in transportation planning and engineering. Most subtly, all buildings and facilities in the new complex were named after longtime, living politicians who had served in the state legislature before and throughout the battles over civil rights and defenses of segregation. The choice avoided historical references and provided politicians an opportunity for self-congratulation on the recently democratized grounds.

Since the 1960s decisions and debates about the form and purpose of the State House grounds have become more public and democratic than any time in their history. No longer only deliberated by

The Capitol Complex in 1979, featuring the recently completed Blatt, Brown, and Gressette Buildings and the entrance to the underground parking garage. Courtesy of Richland Library, Columbia, S.C.

a privileged few, the alteration or addition of monuments increasingly has required compromise among groups that often disagree on everything except the grounds' potential ideological power. Diverse communities throughout the state have demanded representation and revision of the grounds' historical narratives. At the same time, South Carolinians have begun to understand that sponsors' intentions behind a monument can be even more important than the history they purport to celebrate.

James Francis Byrnes Monument

Unveiled 1972
Charles Cropper Parks, sculptor;
Robert E. Marvin, landscape architect

This one and one-half times life-size bronze statue honors James Francis Byrnes (1882–1972), one of South Carolina's most powerful and nationally prominent politician of the twentieth century. Called "a man for all offices" at the monument's televised dedication in 1972, "Jimmy" Byrnes is one of the few Americans to serve in the state government as well as all three branches of the federal government.[2] In setting and composition, the bronze statue contrasts

James Francis Byrnes Monument. Photograph by Chandler Yonkers, 2020.

with that of Byrnes's mentor, Benjamin Tillman, on the other side of the State House grounds. Whereas Tillman's monument stands along the capitol's axis atop a high base, Byrnes's sits thoughtfully in a contemplative and shady corner plaza. The statue was the first on the grounds to be planned while its subject was still alive (although it was dedicated just weeks after his death), and Byrnes had direct input on its design.[3]

Jimmy Byrnes rose from humble beginnings in Charleston to the US House and Senate and a brief appointment as associate justice of the Supreme Court. His powerful White House roles directing wartime economy, labor, and industry under Franklin Delano Roosevelt earned him the nickname "assistant president" that is engraved on the monument's base. As secretary of state under Harry S. Truman, he directed the deployment of the world's first hydrogen bombs at the end of World War II. In his last political position as South Carolina's governor, Byrnes focused on maintaining racial segregation during the legal battle over "separate but equal" public schools.[4]

The effort to memorialize Byrnes "at the height of a mature and distinguished career" began before the reconfiguration and expansion of the State House grounds.[5] Friends and former colleagues, most of whom were involved with Byrnes's educational foundation, established a committee and hired sculptor Charles Cropper Parks in 1963.[6] In accordance with Byrnes's wishes, no public or state funds were used for the sculpture.[7] Textile magnate Roger Milliken donated twice as much money as any other single sponsor; he had benefited immensely from the politician's antilabor policies.[8] The group easily decided upon the prominent corner site because of its location across Sumter Street from Byrnes's grave at Trinity Cathedral and from the Gervais Street post office that would soon house the state's supreme court (the court moved there from the State House in 1971).[9]

Robert E. Marvin, the landscape architect who redesigned the State House grounds in the late 1960s, planned the bell-shaped plaza around existing gingko trees and to coordinate with the grounds' new pathways and city sidewalks. Charles Parks suggested using granite for the base and the cobblestone paving to enhance "the

Charles Parks's clay maquette of the Byrnes statue with a bronze screen featuring the seals of the various branches of government in which Byrnes served (not executed). Courtesy of South Caroliniana Library, University of South Carolina, Columbia, S.C.

unity of the design."[10] Parks had originally planned a large, bronze, semicircular screen to frame the statue featuring seals of all of the branches of government in which Byrnes had served.[11] Although the artist pitched the screen as "an integral part of the scheme," it would have doubled the $30,000 cost of the monument and thus the committee chose not to commission it.[12] Shrubbery was substituted to shield the statue from the street and to define the space's edge.

Like the Sims, Hampton, and Confederate Women's Monuments, which were moved in the same years as its design and execution, the Byrnes statue was oriented to face the State House. Even though Byrnes resigned his lifetime appointment to the US Supreme Court after only two years to serve in Roosevelt's wartime White House, the statue depicts him in "timeless" judicial robes.[13] Byrnes holds a copy of one of his two autobiographies; both books are among the items buried in the time capsule at the statue's base.[14]

Byrnes's wife, Maude, unveiled the monument just two weeks after the politician's death in 1972. The General Assembly dedicated the day to Byrnes and hoped that the statue would "remain in mute testimony for all who pass it by that this is indeed the land of opportunity for those who dare to seek it."[15]

Redesign of the State House Grounds

Designed and executed 1969–72
Robert E. Marvin, landscape architect

Like many of the improvements to the State House grounds before it, the 1969 redesign of the two blocks on which the capitol sits resulted from a confluence of controversies, long-standing frustrations, and practical needs. In the early 1960s local history enthusiasts renewed their interest in the landscape when the widening of Gervais Street threatened to encroach upon the grounds (necessitating the slight move of the Jefferson Davis Memorial Highway marker).[16] Recent renovations of the capitol's interior, meanwhile, offered a stark contrast with the "grease-splattered parking lot" surrounding the Confederate Monument and the "unsightly trash disposal bin" along Assembly Street.[17] Campaign stops by Richard Nixon in 1960 and Lyndon Johnson in 1964 heightened the public's embarrassment over the state of the grounds.[18] By the time long-term planning for new state office buildings began toward the end of the decade—what would become the Capitol Complex—energy had finally galvanized to commission a comprehensive plan for the grounds for the first time since Harlan P. Kelsey's 1904 unrealized master plan. Executed 1969–72, Robert E. Marvin's design is maintained in the

6-A   THE STATE—Columbia, S. C., Thursday, May 23, 1963

How Capitol's Grounds Would Look if Proposal Passes

Rendering by Gil Petroff of the fountain proposed to replace
the parking lot around the Confederate Monument, 1962.
Courtesy of Richland Library, Columbia, S.C.

layout of paths and placement of monuments that visitors see today.

Governor Robert McNair first approached landscape architect Robert E. Marvin about redesigning the State House grounds in 1967.[19] He was especially interested in recent suggestions to replace the parking lot around the Confederate Monument with an elaborate Beaux-Arts fountain.[20] Marvin, a native of rural Colleton County, an advocate for the environment in modern design, and the state's leading landscape design professional, gently advocated instead for a "total design" approach in which "the scope of development for the capital grounds should be settled only after imaginative research into both the use and the aesthetic possibilities of the site."[21] Marvin was hired, a study of the existing landscape begun, and the fountain idea quietly abandoned.

Working closely with Lyles, Bissett, Carlisle & Wolff (LBC&W) and Wilbur Smith & Associates (WS&A), the architecture and engineering firms planning the Capitol Complex at the same time, Robert E. Marvin and Associates redesigned the path system, proposed new locations for existing monuments, and instituted a horticultural

Men enjoying the views of the State House grounds in spring, 1965. Note the pipe railings and irregular walks, removed during the redesign by Robert Marvin. Courtesy of Richland Library, Columbia, S.C.

plan for the grounds north of Senate Street. In contrast to the sparsely planted and largely concrete pedestrian mall of the Capitol Complex, Marvin embraced—but did not restore—the picturesque balance of Otto Schwagerl's plan of the 1870s. He eliminated the sidewalks and pipe railings that had been introduced intermittently over the years and disrupted Schwagerl's plan. He developed a unified, symmetrical system of paths in two concentric loops around the State House with arteries at regular intervals connecting to Sumter, Gervais, and Assembly Streets on the perimeter.

The result, like Marvin's designs for residential projects and Sea Pines Plantation in Hilton Head of the same period, sensitively approached the site's historic context and invited visitors to "wrap [their] arms around nature."[22] Sharply edged paths curve through dense plantings of tall trees, lush bushes, and textured ground cover. He designed the walks and plantings "so that you would not see the streets" and retained mature trees (one example is a large magnolia that sits in the center of a path on the west side).[23] He independently conceived pushing parking underground and closing Senate Street at the same time that LBC&W and WS&A came up with the same idea, freeing the ground level to be a park.[24] He carefully chose a light gray granite aggregate so that the sidewalks would "fit in with the Capitol" and directed the construction team to scatter the crushed rock by hand to ensure that it was "evenly distributed" as the cement dried.[25] Although he did not design the Capitol Complex's pedestrian mall south of Senate Street, Marvin encouraged LBC&W to feature "more greenery and less paved plaza" around the new buildings.[26]

Marvin, LBC&W, and WS&A also collaborated on raising and regularizing the grassy "podium" on which the State House sits, providing a platform "more suitable to its massive size."[27] In consultation with historians at the state archives, Marvin's plan moved the Palmetto Monument and Liberty Bell away from the State House to new sites, focusing attention on the building's architecture and mass. He also relocated the Spanish-American War cannon and the Hampton, Sims, and Confederate Women's Monuments and turned each to face the capitol. The reorganization offered new focal points for the landscape but interrupted the original meanings of the spatial relationships between monuments (such as the axis between the Hampton, Partisan Generals, and Tillman Monuments with Trinity Cathedral).

Capitol Complex Master Plan

Designed 1969
Lyles, Bissett, Carlisle & Wolff, architects and planners;
Wilbur Smith & Associates, engineers

The Capitol Complex covers the two blocks south of the State House and includes the Blatt, Brown, Gressette, and Dennis Buildings; the

McEachern Parking Garage; and the pedestrian mall that replaced these blocks of Main and Senate Streets. This massive addition to the State House grounds was conceived in the late 1960s to respond to a variety of long-festering needs for office space, which peaked thanks to the expansion of state government under Governor Robert McNair.

The newly formed Division of General Services assumed control over construction, maintenance, and purchasing for all state buildings in 1964, centralizing responsibility for the State House grounds under a single agency for the first time. It began in 1967 with land acquisition surrounding the State House, a parking study by engineering outfit Wilbur Smith & Associates and comprehensive plans by architecture firm Lyles, Bissett, Carlisle & Wolff.[28] The effort was the first attempt by the state government to plan for its spatial needs in the long-term, differentiating it from earlier stop-gap measures such as the stand-alone Calhoun, Hampton, and Rutledge State Office Buildings or the parking lot that long surrounded the Confederate Monument. It was completed with the dedication of the Dennis Building in 1981.

The Capitol Complex's stark Brutalist architecture and rigid symmetry are distinct from the rich surfaces of the State House and its picturesque grounds. Its logical organization and modern style suggest the rationality and fiscal restraint of the bureaucracy housed therein and complements—but does not compete—with the bold classicism of the State House. The pedestrian mall forms a strong axis from the south steps of the State House and preserves both the footprint of the block of Main Street that it replaced and views to and from the capitol. Because the topography of the site slopes away from the State House, the complex's southern edge along Pendleton Street sits above street level on a platform created by the parking garage beneath. The buildings (all planned by LBC&W) are unified in their height, limestone façades, and architectural style. Their material palette and scale also coordinate with the Calhoun and Hampton Buildings of the 1920s and '30s.

The Capitol Complex was constructed between 1969 and 1981 according to plans drawn for its first phase. Working together,

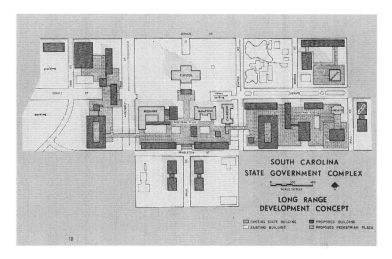

LBC&W with WS&A, Capitol Complex master plan, 1969.
Note the pedestrian mall that extended to buildings across Assembly
and Sumter Streets. Courtesy of South Caroliniana Library,
University of South Carolina, Columbia, S.C.

LBC&W and WS&A closed portions of Senate and Main Streets to create a pedestrian mall; retained the Highway Building (remodeled and renamed for Rembert Dennis) and the Hampton and Calhoun Buildings; suggested the matching Brown and Blatt Buildings along Pendleton Street and the Marion Gressette Building just east of the Highway Building on Senate Street; and buried parking in an underground garage.[29]

Later phases of the master plan were never completed. They imagined a network of pedestrian malls connecting the Capitol Complex to new government buildings to the south along Main Street (recalling the Beaux-Arts arrangement of the Kelsey plan), west across Assembly Street, and east along Senate Street to the Rutledge Building and State Archives.[30] William G. Lyles, a founding partner of LBC&W, told the governor: "our first consideration is filling functional needs at reasonable cost—but hopefully in a manner that will complement our existing buildings and tie this area together into an efficient, pleasant, and beautiful development in which we may all be justifiably proud."[31] Although the state did construct a handful of additional buildings to the east and west in the following decade (including the state library on Senate Street and a parking garage on Assembly Street), they were never joined to the State House grounds by pedestrian malls.

Construction on the Capitol Complex began with the underground parking garage and the LBC&W-designed modular energy facility at Main and College Streets (connected to the complex via tunnels) in 1969–70.[32] But persistent budget hawks in the legislature, mounting public criticism, and the mid-1970s recession ultimately prevented the Capitol Complex's full realization. Opposition dubbed it the "Deficit Spending Bill of 1968" and saw it as a dangerous manifestation of the government's ever-expanding "vast bureaucracy."[33] Concerns over the fiscal scale of the project (and especially the furnishing of the Blatt Building) also severely curtailed the implementation of the pedestrian mall, cutting the installation of fountains and groups of trees and substituting sand clay for quality topsoil on the roof of the parking garage.[34]

Lyles, Bissett, Carlisle & Wolff

Incorporated by William G. Lyles, Thomas J. Bissett, William A. Carlisle, and Louis M. Wolff in 1948, LBC&W was the state's largest and most successful architecture firm by the late 1960s. The firm designed in all guises of modernism: International Style (including the Banker's Trust Tower, across Gervais Street from the State House grounds), New Formalism (including the Thomas Cooper Library on UofSC's campus with Edward Durrell Stone), and Brutalism. The firm shuttered just as it completed the Capitol Complex in the late 1970s. The Dennis Building's renovation, planned in the same style and materials as the rest of LBC&W's buildings, was completed by successor firm McNair, Gordon, Johnson & Karasiewicz.

LBC&W had considerable experience executing government contracts and knew how to navigate the bureaucracy and budget restraints of state institutions. It built more than fifty thousand housing units with Federal Housing Authority funding in the 1940s and 1950s, including the Cornell Arms and Claire Tower apartment buildings just across from the Capitol Complex on Pendleton and Senate Streets, respectively.[35] It was the leading architecture firm for buildings on state university campuses (including Clemson House and Cooper Library at Clemson and Russell House and Sumwalt at UofSC). In 1966 the firm completed its first building for the state's newly created Division of General Services: the 87,731-square-foot Rutledge Building.[36] Just a few blocks east of the State House on Senate Street, the bold $3.5 million glass-and-marble tower proclaimed the ambitions of the state and addressed the never-ending shortage of office space on the State House grounds. It sat across from the recently completed state archives, forming a new nucleus for state buildings that the firm hoped would be connected to the Capitol Complex with a pedestrian mall in a later phase of construction. Although it successfully helped to convince the state to hire LBC&W to design the Capitol Complex, the Rutledge Building was never directly connected to the State House grounds.[37]

Columbia's Master Plan and Wilbur Smith & Associates

The Capitol Complex fit into LBC&W's master plan for downtown Columbia, an ambitious attempt to accommodate a growing population through large-scale urban renewal and comprehensive planning that promised to "eliminate the slums, provide decent housing for the poor, and make the city a more desirable place for the affluent."[38] In the late 1960s LBC&W coordinated with WS&A and the internationally renowned planner Constantinos Doxiadis to reimagine how Columbia could remain functional and dynamic for the next thirty years. Their "Mall of Main Street" would have transformed the city's main commercial avenue into a pedestrian mall "spine" lined by new, ten-story modern buildings and connecting the capitol to a massive city/county government complex to the north at Blanding Street.[39] The most lasting effects of the Doxiadis/LBC&W plan are the Richland County Courthouse and the destruction of the African American neighborhood of Ward I for UofSC's expansion.

LBC&W and WS&A had a close relationship prior to their cooperation on the Capitol Complex and the Columbia Master Plan:

they had partnered on the siting and parking plans for UofSC's Carolina Coliseum and the International Style post office on Assembly Street. The firms also leased office space alongside one another in the LBC&W-designed Banker's Trust Tower when it opened across from the capitol in the mid-1970s.[40] Begun by Columbia brothers Wilbur and James Smith, WS&A had designed and studied highways, shopping centers, housing complexes, airports, bridges, and infrastructure systems on six continents by the time it joined forces with LBC&W for the Capitol Complex.[41] The firm had also worked closely with Constantinos Doxiadis before the city of Columbia hired him for its master plan.

Furman McEachern Jr. Parking Garage

Built 1971–78
Lyles, Bissett, Carlisle & Wolff, architects and planners;
Wilbur Smith & Associates, engineers

State officials began discussing an underground garage as early as 1963 to address the lack of parking for the growing number of state employees and the unsightly surface lot surrounding the Confederate Monument.[42] The parking garage that resulted became a key component of the massive Capitol Complex that dominates the south end of the State House grounds. Built in two phases between 1969 and 1978, the garage hides parking for 1,812 cars and forms a concrete platform for the Blatt and Brown Buildings and the pedestrian mall that surrounds them.

Self-park underground garages first appeared in select American cities in the 1930s and were commonplace across the country by the 1950s and '60s.[43] LBC&W and WS&A began to study and design for coordinated underground parking facilities and state office buildings in Columbia in 1967, and the legislature funded the first phase of

The parking garage under construction in 1970 south of the Calhoun Building. Note the building where the Gressette Building now stands. Courtesy of Richland Library, Columbia, S.C.

their plan for the Capitol Complex the next year.[44] The project was the result of "urban environmental design" that ensured that "highways, parking, and pedestrian amenities . . . [would] mesh with the buildings and land uses in a coordinated manner."[45]

LBC&W and WS&A spread the garage's 286,281 square feet across three levels and promised that the facility could empty within a half hour on an average weekday.[46] The first phase was finished beneath the Blatt Building in 1971 while the second was completed between the capitol and the Dennis Building in 1978.[47] The garage forms a lightning bolt shape that connects perpendicularly to Assembly and Senate Streets northwest of the Dennis Building, turns south at the capitol to follow the pedestrian mall above and open onto Main Street, then cuts east to join with the basements of the Brown, Hampton, and Calhoun Buildings. An escalator running beneath the south steps of the State House attaches the garage with the capitol's historic lower lobby.[48] Thus, employees in buildings on the grounds may travel from their cars to their offices without going outside, often leaving the ground level of the Capitol Complex to feel empty of pedestrians. The Pendleton Street entrance was changed and entry restricted to address security concerns in 2007.[49] Additional concrete exits emerge throughout the complex.

Legislators and private citizens criticized the project's cost, apparent extravagances, and seemingly endless construction. They questioned the necessity of the intercom system, which played music throughout the complex, and despairingly dubbed it a "$5.5 million hole in the ground."[50] Governor Robert McNair's staff later remembered that "when they started digging the big hole [his] political opponents said they were going to bury Bob in it."[51] Even though plans to extend the garage were scrapped, the final project cost was still $11 million.[52]

In 1979–80, the legislature named the parking garage after Furman McEachern Jr. (1920–80), who oversaw the construction of the Capitol Complex. A native of Jenkinsville, he began his career in the state Highway Department and then served as the first director of the Division of General Services, which created more than 1.25 million square feet of office space across the state during his tenure. McEachern died the week before the parking garage was dedicated in honor of him as a "moving force who made state government effective and responsive during its greatest period of growth."[53]

Edgar A. Brown Building and Solomon Blatt Building

Brown Building, built 1971–73
Lyles, Bissett, Carlisle & Wolff, architects

Blatt Building, built 1975–79
Lyles, Bissett, Carlisle & Wolff, architects

These "twin" state office buildings anchor the southern edge of the Capitol Complex along Pendleton Street. Their arrangement on either side of the complex's pedestrian mall allow for an "unhindered vista of the Capitol."[54] The Brown Building was completed in 1973 and the Blatt Building followed six years later. Hubert D. Simmons of LBC&W designed the buildings to house office space for a number of state agencies, including the newly created Division of Parks, Recreation, and Tourism. Initially imagined to be seven stories, they were reduced to five after the legislature scaled back the Capitol Complex project shortly after it was initiated.

The two buildings are monumental in scale and Brutalist in style. Their buff limestone sheathing, symmetrical façades, and classical proportions were designed "in keeping with the design and period

Senator Edgar Brown in front of the building named after him at its 1972 dedication. Brown died weeks later. Courtesy of Richland Library, Columbia, S.C.

of the architecture of the State House" and Calhoun and Hampton Buildings.[55] Their identical north and south sides and glass lobbies signal the transparency of government and communicate that visitors can enter from any side. Like all office buildings built as part of the master plan, the repetitive rows of windows on each of the buildings' exterior faces suggest the individual offices that line the interior, adhering to modern architecture's dictum that the form of a building must follow its function.

The General Assembly named the buildings after state legislators who had long-represented Barnwell County and were central to the funding and planning of the Capitol Complex. The Brown Building was a "tribute in concrete" to recently retired senator Edgar Allan Brown (1888–1975), who died from injuries sustained in a car accident just two weeks after the building's dedication.[56] A Democrat known as the "Bishop of Barnwell," Brown had served in the General Assembly from 1920 until 1972, including thirty years as the powerful president pro tempore of the Senate. He also chaired Clemson University's Board of Trustees during its court-ordered integration and introduced the legislation naming the state's previous office buildings after Wade Hampton and John C. Calhoun in 1940.[57] The Blatt Building was named after Solomon Blatt (1895–1986), a conservative who served in the state legislature from 1930 until 1973, including thirty-two years as Speaker of the House. A lawyer, Blatt was a proponent of industrial development throughout his career.

L. Marion Gressette Building

Built 1975–78

Lyles, Bissett, Carlisle & Wolff, architects

The square L. Marion Gressette Building fits neatly in a corner formed by the Capitol Complex's pedestrian mall and the pre-existing Dennis Building. Together with the Dennis, Hampton, and

L. Marion Gressette Building. Note that the treatment of the
first floor is different from the Brown and Blatt Buildings.
Photograph by Chandler Yonkers, 2020.

Calhoun Buildings, it sits at a deferential distance from the historic
State House and preserves the edge of what was once Senate Street.
The Gressette Building's Brutalist, symmetrical, limestone exterior
references the other structures built in the 1970s as part of the Capitol Complex. Planned as an office building for state legislators, it
features suites of offices on the first floor. This differs from the glass
lobbies along the first floors of the Blatt and Brown Buildings, which
are more visually inviting to citizens who might be visiting the various state agencies housed in the stories above.

Although LBC&W had imagined a structure on this site from its
earliest plans for the Capitol Complex, a faltering economy, debates
over spending, and the fact that it was built to house offices for legislators made it controversial by the time bulldozers started digging
its foundation in 1975.[58] Some legislators initially refused to occupy
their assigned offices when the building was finished, despite the
fact that they and their staffs were crammed into every "crowded
corner" of the State House.[59] These politicians protested that "the

expenditure for the buildings and reports of purchases of plush furniture for some offices [were] weighing heavy on the public mind."[60]

At the building's dedication in February 1979, legislators ultimately declared that it was as "strong, noble and tall" as the person for whom they named it, Calhoun County legislator Lawrence Marion Gressette (1902–84).[61] Gressette served in the House and Senate from 1925 until 1984 as a conservative who fought for decades against desegregation. Hailing the building as a "steel and concrete symbol of the long and durable legislative service of its namesake," speakers at the dedicatory ceremony disregarded the senator's early opposition to the expense of the Capitol Complex.[62]

Rembert C. Dennis Building

Built 1952, renovated 1978–81
Lyles, Bissett, Carlisle & Wolff and
McNair, Gordon, Johnson & Karasiewicz, architects

Florence architecture firm Hopkins, Baker & Gill designed this steel structure for the South Carolina Highway Department thirty years before it was gutted and sheathed with a new its Brutalist exterior to match the other structures of the Capitol Complex in 1979–81. An earlier iteration of the firm had designed the Wade Hampton State Office Building in the 1930s. Sitting on what was then Senate Street in line with the Hampton and Calhoun Buildings, the Highway Building's "modernistic" International Style differed dramatically from the Classical Revival architecture of its neighbors but referenced the modernity and efficiency of the state's new road infrastructure.[63] When the "License Plate" building opened in 1952, it consolidated 450 workers scattered over fifteen different buildings and featured a restaurant and large open drafting rooms for producing drawings of state infrastructure.[64] An addition was made in the following decade to create the building's doughnut-shaped footprint.

The South Carolina Highway Department Building in 1961,
later remodeled and renamed for Rembert C. Dennis. Note the
Calhoun and Hampton Buildings to the east along Senate Street.
Courtesy of Richland Library, Columbia, S.C.

Rembert C. Dennis Building. Photograph by Chandler Yonkers, 2020.

The state purchased the building from the Highway Department, an income-generating division of state government, in 1973. The Highway Department then used the proceeds to build new facilities on Park Street in downtown Columbia and outside the city on Shop Road.[65] Many argued that renovation of the building for office space would cost as much as—if not more than—a new structure and that "monetary considerations cannot be forfeited on purely aesthetic grounds, particularly when tax monies are involved." The ongoing controversy over funding for the Blatt and Gressette Buildings only fueled such opposition.[66]

Ultimately calling the building a "retrofit," McNair, Gordon, Johnson & Karasiewicz, a successor architecture firm to LBC&W, stripped the building down to its steel frame, added an additional story (included in the original plans for the structure but never built), rearranged its interiors for offices, maintained the interior courtyard, and covered the exteriors with limestone to maintain "architectural consistency" with the rest of the Capitol Complex.[67]

Outfitted with office space for state agencies and officials, it was formally dedicated to Berkeley County Democrat Rembert Coney Dennis (1915–92) in 1981. Dennis was about to retire after having worked almost fifty years in the General Assembly and as the third generation of his family to serve in the legislature. Dennis proclaimed that the placement of the building next to one named after L. Marion Gressette was a fitting "testimony" to his friendship with his fellow fiscal conservative.[68] A striking full-length relief sculpture of Dennis by local artist and art educator Jean McWhorter adorns the lobby on the north side of the building. It is more elaborate than the simple bronze busts of Gressette, Brown, and Blatt in the lobbies of their respective buildings.[69]

Richardson Square Marker

Dedicated 1972

The General Assembly designated the space between the State House's south steps and the Gressette Building as "Richardson Square" in 1972.[70] Closed to vehicular traffic as part of the Capitol Complex's development, the space honor Richard Richardson (ca. 1705–80), an early state legislator, Revolutionary War militia general, and immediate ancestor of six subsequent governors of the state.[71] Initiated by one of his descendants then serving in the state legislature, the square also references the original name for the capital city's Main Street: Richardson Street.[72] The city's 1786 plan called for a number of north–south streets to be named after Revolutionary War generals, including Richardson, Andrew Pickens, Thomas Sumter, and Francis Marion (the last three also recognized in the grounds' Partisan General's Monument), but Columbians often substituted "Main" for "Richardson" in the nineteenth century before forgoing the name entirely by the end of the 1890s.[73] The Columbia

Richardson Square Marker. Photograph by Chandler Yonkers, 2020.

Committee of the National Society of the Colonial Dames of America in the State of South Carolina installed a plaque with Richardson's portrait and biography in 1976.[74] A song traditionally played by the Richardson family was adopted as the state waltz in 2000.

Capitol Complex Marker

Dedicated 1981
Karkadoulias Bronze Art and Jean McWhorter, sculptors

This marker dedicates the Capitol Complex to Robert Evander McNair, a lawyer and Democratic governor of South Carolina. During

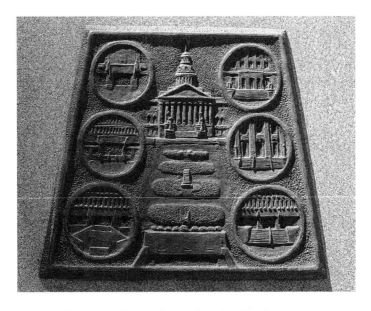

Detail of the Capitol Complex Marker, showing the State House, Confederate Women's Monument, and the marker itself. Photograph by Chandler Yonkers, 2020.

his administration from 1965 to 1971, McNair oversaw the planning and initial construction of the two-block complex, negotiated the desegregation of the state's public schools and universities, and founded the state's Department of Parks, Recreation and Tourism. He later took responsibility for highway patrol officers shooting unarmed African Americans protesting segregation at South Carolina State University on February 8, 1968, known as the "Orangeburg Massacre."[75]

Dedicated in 1981 just months after the Dennis Building, this marker was the final piece of the Capitol Complex to be built. The relief sculpture by Jean McWhorter on one side pictures each of the complex's buildings and even represents the monument itself along the pedestrian mall. McNair recognized at the ceremony that he remained "in the same place I've always been, in the shadow" of senior legislators Brown, Blatt, Gressette, and Dennis, for whom the buildings of the complex were named.[76] Interestingly, the marker misstates the dates of construction for the Rembert C. Dennis Building. The building was originally constructed in 1952 and renovated in 1979–81. The dedicatory plaque in the Dennis Building's lobby repeats the error, likely attesting to the fact that the renovated building retains only its original steel structure and doughnut-shaped footprint.[77]

Columbia Bicentennial Time Capsule

Dedicated 1986

A granite marker rests atop a two-foot square steel time capsule commemorating the city of Columbia's two hundredth birthday in 1986.[78] The burial of the capsule culminated a year of public celebrations, neighborhood festivals, parades, and documentation projects.

With the theme "Looking Back—Reaching Forward," the city hoped that the bicentennial effort would "provide citizens a focus on what their city has been and what it can be" and highlight new developments such as the Congaree Vista, the Koger Center for the Performing Arts, and the reinvigoration of the city's waterfront.[79] The capsule includes letters from over one hundred citizens, newspaper clippings, and materials from the city's 1936 sesquicentennial. It will be opened at the city's semiquincentennial, on May 22, 2036 (its 250th birthday).[80]

Columbia Bicentennial Time Capsule Marker.
Photograph by Chandler Yonkers, 2020.

Strom Thurmond Monument. Photograph by Chandler Yonkers, 2020.

Strom Thurmond Monument

Dedicated 1999
William Behrends, sculptor

Placed prominently on the southern axis of the Capitol Complex's pedestrian mall, the statue of James Strom Thurmond (1902–2003) joins the other monuments on the State House grounds that represent individual politicians (Jimmy Byrnes, Wade Hampton, and Benjamin Ryan Tillman). The nine-foot-tall bronze sculpture depicts the oldest and one of the longest-serving US senators in American history striding confidently atop an eight-foot-tall pedestal.[81]

An Edgefield native, Thurmond began his career as a lawyer, state senator, and judge. After returning home from World War II, he was elected to one term as governor before serving in the US Senate from

1956 until 2003. He ran against Harry Truman in the 1948 presidential election as a candidate for the States' Rights Democratic Party (often called the Dixiecrats), a political party organized to resist federal civil rights legislation. He devoted decades of his career to preventing racial integration, and his twenty-four-hour filibuster in the Senate against the Civil Rights Act of 1957 still holds the record for the longest in American history. Thurmond argued throughout his life that he was motivated by concerns over states' rights rather than racism, although he refashioned himself at the end of his career as a conservative with more inclusive views.[82]

The campaign for the Thurmond Monument was the second on the State House grounds begun while its subject was still alive (Byrnes was the first). Soon after Thurmond's last election in 1997, the General Assembly easily passed legislation creating a commission of legislators to decide on a monument.[83] State senator and former Thurmond aide John Courson, then advocating to keep the

Detail of the Thurmond Monument showing the addition of Essie Mae Washington-Williams's name. Photograph by Chandler Yonkers, 2020.

Confederate flag on the grounds, was a leader for the project.[84] The commission considered thirteen proposals that featured Thurmond in a range of ages and poses but ultimately chose sculptor William Behrends's depiction of Thurmond shortly after winning his first Senate election in 1954.[85]

Like the Byrnes statue, the monument was privately and quickly funded. Individuals made small donations, but 62 percent of the statue's final $850,000 price tag came from the seven corporate sponsors inscribed on its base.[86] Many noticed—and African American legislators commented—that the monument's planning, fundraising, and construction outpaced the African American History Monument, which had been in the works since 1994. Senator Darrell Jackson noted, "With all due respect to Sen. Thurmond, I think that this gives the impression that one man is more important than a whole race of people," while Representative Gilda Cobb-Hunter recognized that "you don't have to be a rocket scientist to come up with a statue to him. You do have to put up a lot of work to come up with an appropriate monument to a people."[87] The 1999 dedication was coordinated with Thurmond's ninety-seventh birthday.[88] He told the 1,200 people attending the ceremony: "It is my hope in years to come young South Carolinians will look at this statue and other statues that grace these beautiful grounds and ask themselves, 'How can I make a difference? How can I serve?'"[89]

Within months of the senator's 2003 death, Essie Mae Washington-Williams came forward and revealed herself to be Thurmond's daughter. Thurmond had fathered Washington-Williams with his family's African American maid in 1925 and had secretly supported her throughout his life.[90] The legislature unanimously decided to add her name to the monument's base to join those of Thurmond's other children, along with the change of the number of his children from "four" to "five." Both Black and White legislators supported the change, seeing her as a "class act" and respectful of Thurmond's legacy.[91] Washington-Williams's name and the corrected number of children were sandblasted onto the side of the monument without ceremony in 2004.[92]

African American History Monument.
Photograph by Chandler Yonkers, 2020.

African American History Monument

Dedicated 2001
Ed Dwight, sculptor

The African American History Monument tells a long and uplifting story of Black peoples' experiences in South Carolina from ca. 1670 to the present day. The monument is the largest and most narratively ambitious on the State House grounds: rather than honoring a single person or event, it tells a story about millions of people over hundreds of years. The process to build this monument was equally complex and surely the most inclusive of any in the history of the site. Unlike the self-selected group of legislators or private individuals that organized the other monuments, the African American History Monument's planning involved hundreds of South Carolinians across the state. With such a broad narrative, smaller figures, and partially enclosed footprint, the monument creates its own space for storytelling and contemplation. While it celebrates the very people that many of the people memorialized elsewhere on the grounds spent their lives oppressing, it does not directly confront these other monuments in its design or narrative.

The idea for a monument recognizing "the unique experiences and contributions of African-Americans in this state" originated in 1994 as debates intensified over whether the Confederate battle flag should fly atop the State House.[93] Protests and threats of boycotts and lawsuits pressured legislators to devise a compromise that would appease both those who saw the flag as a symbol of heritage and those for whom it represented bigotry and injustice. Many interpreted the proposed monument as a "quid pro quo" exchange for allowing the flag to remain, a means to privilege the history of White peoples' defense of slavery alongside the first recognition of Black South Carolinians on the State House grounds.[94] The compromise failed, and after prolonged debate in 1996, the General Assembly created a commission, granted a site, and mandated that all funding for the African American History Monument be raised privately.[95] The flag was relocated from the top of the capitol's dome to the Confederate Monument in 2000 and removed from the grounds entirely in 2015.[96]

Although the legislature ultimately separated the flag and monument, many continued to regard them as closely tied issues. The legislature chose White state senator Glenn McConnell, a major defender of the Confederate flag, to lead the legislative monument commission. Representative Gilda Cobb-Hunter, the commission's vice chair and an African American woman, argued that the monument and the flag were separate concerns.[97] Cobb-Hunter recognized the power of the monument's location adjacent to the State House, a building constructed by enslaved men: "When you look at the role of the slaves and the roles that slaves played in the building of this country, clearly, it's going to be remarkable."[98]

After soliciting public comments, the commission invited proposals for the monument that were representational, not limited
to a single figure, and told the long history of Black South Carolinians through a series of historical scenes. A design by Ed Dwight, a
Colorado-based sculptor and NASA's first African American astronaut candidate, won over the other forty-six entries in the monument competition in part because it promised to fit in with existing
monuments.[99]

Dwight devised the monument to sit in its own semicircular
plaza that sets itself apart from the rest of the grounds. This creates
a distinct space facing away from the State House, much like the
Law Enforcement Memorial (first designed in 1994) and the South
Carolina Vietnam Veterans Memorial (erected in Columbia's Memorial Park in 1986).[100] It begins its chronological narrative in Africa via
the plaza's semicircular shape (Dwight meant to recall the footprint
of an African village), a twenty-three-foot-tall obelisk (a form understood to have originated in Egypt), four stones and a map indicating
the places from which Africans were kidnapped, and the representation of a slave ship in bronze and terrazzo.[101] Arranged chronologically flanking the obelisk, bronze relief sculptures depict scenes of
African Americans' enslavement, freedom, struggle for civil rights,
and contemporary achievements. The first panel on the north side
offers the only positive representation of Reconstruction-era African Americans on the State House grounds, thus quietly countering
many monuments that memorialize the state as something to be "redeemed" from Black power by Wade Hampton and his successors.

The commission spent three years debating the monument's con-
tent, disagreeing especially on which historic figures to depict and
how or whether to present moments of struggle and violence.[102] In
order to avoid controversy and to ensure the legislature's approval of
the final design, some of the monument's supporters sought to "talk
about black endurance in the face of oppression, not about who was
doing the oppressing."[103] For the panel on the Jim Crow era (the period in which most of the grounds' monuments were built), Dwight
had originally imagined "hooded Klansmen burning crosses and the
bodies of blacks hanging from trees," but the commission "asked him

Detail of the Reconstruction and Jim Crow panels on the African American History Monument. Photograph by Chandler Yonkers, 2020.

to tone it down, saying the images would become a lightning rod of controversy."[104] The design ultimately depicted the period through a series of words. The commission also specifically rejected the representation of Denmark Vesey, a free African American man who led a slave revolt in Charleston in 1822.[105] It specified that no individuals were to be commemorated, though many recognize specific examples in the monument's final panel, including South Carolina's first licensed female physician, Dr. Matilda Evans; the first African American chief justice on the South Carolina Supreme Court since Reconstruction, Ernest Finney Jr.; astronaut Ronald McNair; politician Jesse Jackson; musician Dizzy Gillespie; boxer Joe Frazier; and the first African American to win a Grand Slam tennis title, Althea Gibson.[106]

At the monument's 2001 dedication, poet Nikky Finney (daughter of Chief Justice Finney) said, "Embrace your history . . . not just the pretty things." She read her poem, written for the event:

We were never slaves—we were enslaved,

A people who fought and remained free in
our own minds, free to imagine more than
others imagined for us,

Walk through these bronzed determined faces
and you will find raised arms and the histories
of a people with different free things on their
minds, at different times,

Althea Gibson, born just up the road in Silver,
South Carolina, is there with a million black
forearms swinging with her, Wimbledon 1957,

Matilda Arabella Evans, first woman physician
in Columbia, first Black woman physician in
South Carolina, who took care of anyone who
needed her, no matter their color,

Walk through and remember all the houses
down by Daufuskie, with every roof and
windowsill painted African blue, for added
protection,

Walk through and see the bare dirt yards swept
clean, all across the state, each morning, by Black
hands that made sea grass stick brooms that could
sweep the dirt and the worry away,

See the sea-shelled decorated graves holding the
faces of old phones and clocks that push out of
the grave-bed like personal jewelry, a reminder
of what time Mama crossed over,

Walk through these lives and you will find
every Black church ever built in South Carolina,
still on its knees, still praying, for better days,
better days.[107]

As specified in the law that established the commission, private funds paid entirely for the $1.2 million monument. Automobile manufacturer BMW and the state's Legislative Black Caucus each offered the maximum donation of $25,000, but many private individuals made more modest contributions (including students at W. G. Sanders Middle School in Columbia who donated $505 in change).[108]

South Carolina Law Enforcement Memorial and Armed Forces Monument

Dedicated 2005 and 2006

Dedicated within months of each other in 2005–6, the South Carolina Law Enforcement Memorial and South Carolina Armed Forces Monument create distinct spaces on the State House grounds. Along with the African American History Monument—dedicated in 2001—they are the largest monuments on the State House grounds and use similar circular designs. Unlike the privately funded African American Monument, however, both were paid for almost entirely with taxpayer money appropriated by the legislature. All three were conceived amid the height of debates over the role of the Confederate flag on the grounds. They were the last monuments added before the General Assembly passed a law limiting future monument construction in 2007.

South Carolina Law Enforcement Memorial

Robert P. Young, designer

The South Carolina Law Enforcement Memorial honors officers killed in the line of duty since 1797. A "thin blue line" symbolizes "the concept of the police as a barrier between citizens and crime" and leads to a forty-five-foot-wide circular plaza and a fourteen-foot-tall pillar topped by an eagle.[109] Five granite tablets with officers' names line the perimeter and form the shape of a star.

Michael Loftis, the executive director of the South Carolina Lodge of the Fraternal Order of Police, led the effort for a statewide memorial to law enforcement officers.[110] The project came on the heels of the dedication of the National Law Enforcement Memorial in Washington, DC, in 1991, the record-setting deaths of ten police officers in South Carolina over the course of 1992, and a number of local police monuments erected throughout the country following the police beating of Rodney King and the riots and acquittal of the perpetrators that followed in Los Angeles in 1991–92.[111] In 1994 the General Assembly approved a memorial "dedicated to the men and women who serve as law enforcement and corrections officers within the State of South Carolina and will serve as a location where family, friends, and the general public can go to reflect on the ultimate sacrifice that these heroes paid for protecting the citizens of the state."[112] The state's Division of General Services chose the site southwest of the State House and a concept by memorial and granite designer Robert P. Young.[113]

Police officers and their families began a foundation to collect funds for the monument, but fundraising was slow-going. Anxious to see the memorial completed—especially following the successful dedication of the African American History Monument—legislators dedicated $500,000 from the Department of Public Safety's budget to the project in 2002. Governor Mark Sanford vetoed the bill, saying that he couldn't support spending public funds on the memorial "due to the current state budget crisis" and that the monument should be paid for privately.[114] The legislature overturned

South Carolina Law Enforcement Memorial.
Photograph by Chandler Yonkers, 2020.

his veto, began construction according to Young's design in 2005, and dedicated the monument in February 2006.[115] Elaine Jones, the sister of fallen officer Alvin S. Glenn, said at the dedication: "What happened to my brother is something you wish would never happen again. My hope is that everybody who sees this monument would do as much as they can to prevent it from happening."[116]

The monument was initially inscribed with 308 names.[117] New names are periodically added, and the Fraternal Order of Police holds annual candlelight vigils at the monument to recognize those who have died over the course of that year. In 2019 the memorial featured the names of more than four hundred officers.[118]

South Carolina Armed Forces Monument

The South Carolina Armed Forces Monument honors all of the state's military veterans with a forty-two-foot-wide plaza, six twenty-foot poles featuring the flags of the five branches of the armed forces and those who are prisoners of war or missing in action, and an additional thirty-foot pole flying the South Carolina and American

The South Carolina Armed Forces Monument was designed to look like a fort from Assembly Street. Photograph by Chandler Yonkers, 2020.

flags. The seals of each of the military branches are engraved in the bench on the plaza's opposite side. From Assembly Street, the monument's granite wall gives "the perception of a fort . . . to symbolize the protection the military has afforded Americans."[119]

John Courson, a White Republican senator, and Darrell Jackson, a Black Democratic senator, first proposed a "military commons" of flags honoring various branches as part of the compromise to remove the Confederate flag from the State House dome in the spring of 2000. They suggested that the Confederate flag should be placed alongside the Confederate Monument and that such a plaza could provide "military context" for the obelisk. The flag was removed from the dome and installed at the Confederate Monument a few months later without the plaza of flags.[120]

Courson, who had served in the Marines, continued to advocate for a monument that would "serve as a thank-you to the thousands of South Carolinians who have served in the military."[121] Galvanized by the nationwide enthusiasm for military monuments (including the Lexington County Veterans Monument and the World War II Monument on the National Mall) and the surge of patriotism following the terrorist attacks of September 11, 2001, the legislature formed a commission, appropriated $250,000, and chose the Assembly Street location and austere design for the monument by the end of 2002.[122] Courson penned its simple inscription, and it was dedicated on Veteran's Day in November 2005.[123]

Throughout the construction of the Armed Forces Monument and South Carolina Law Enforcement Memorial and following his advocacy for the statue of Strom Thurmond, John Courson also led the charge for a moratorium on future monuments on the State House grounds. He argued that "we don't want the State House to look like a theme park" and "I don't see how you could have any more . . . without having too many."[124] In 2007 the legislature passed a bill that established "a moratorium on the placement of new monuments on the state house grounds" and specified restrictive conditions under which new monuments could be proposed and built.[125] This is the first and only law to dictate any process by which new monuments are established on the grounds.

Appendix

Maps of the South Carolina State House Grounds, 1790–present

KEY FOR ALL MAPS

Buildings

A   State House (1856–1903)

B   Trinity Cathedral (b. 1847)

C   John C. Calhoun State Office Building (1926)

D   Wade Hampton State Office Building (1938)

E   Highway Department Building / Rembert C. Dennis Building (1952; renovated 1978–81)

F   Edgar A. Brown Building (1971–73)

G   Solomon Blatt Building (1975–79)

H   L. Marion Gressette Building (1975–78)

I   Furman McEachern Jr. Parking Garage (1971–78)

Monuments

1   Swanson Lunsford Grave (buried 1799, marker 1837–present)

2   Palmetto Monument (1972–present)

   2a   Palmetto Monument (1854–74)

   2b   Palmetto Monument (1874–78)

   2c   Palmetto Monument (1878–1972)

3   George Washington Monument (1911–present)

   3a   George Washington Monument (inside building 1864–89)

   3b   George Washington Monument (1889–1911)

4   Henry Kirke Brown sculpture (installed by 1861)

5   Confederate Monument (1889–present)

   5a   Confederate Monument (1879–89)

6   Wade Hampton Monument (1969–present)

   6a   Wade Hampton Monument (1906–69)

7   Partisan Generals Monument (1913–present)

8 Confederate Women's Monument (1972–present)

    8a   Confederate Women's Monument (1912–35)

    8b   Confederate Women's Monument (1935–72)

9 Sims Monument (1969–present)

    9a   Sims Monument (1929–69)

10 Jefferson Davis Memorial Highway Marker (ca. 1962–present)

    10a   Jefferson Davis Memorial Highway Marker (moved here from Taylor Street in 1940s–ca. 1962)

11 Robert E. Lee Memorial Highway Marker (1938)

12 George Washington Elms/Tribute Grove (1930s)

13 Stars on State House (1928–present, plaques added and replaced 1936)

14 Old State House Marker (ca. 1969–present)

    14a   Old State House Marker (1938–ca. 1969)

15 Benjamin Ryan Tillman Monument (1940–present)

16 Spanish-American War Veterans Monument (1941–present)

17 Mount for Spanish Cannon (1962–present)

    17a   Mount for Spanish Cannon (1900–62, cannon scrapped 1942)

18 Gun from USS *Maine* (1931–present)

19 Liberty Bell Replica (ca. 1973–present)

    19a   Liberty Bell Replica (1950–ca. 1973)

20 James Francis Byrnes Monument (1972–present)

21 Richardson Square Marker (1976–present)

22 Capitol Complex Marker (1981–present)

23 Columbia Bicentennial Time Capsule (1986–present)

24 Strom Thurmond Monument (1999–present)

25 African American History Monument (2001–present)

26 South Carolina Law Enforcement Memorial (2005–present)

27 South Carolina Armed Forces Monument (2006–present)

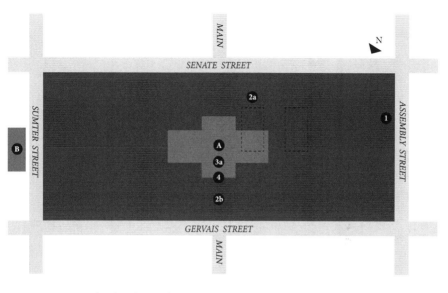

The South Carolina State House Grounds, 1790–1877

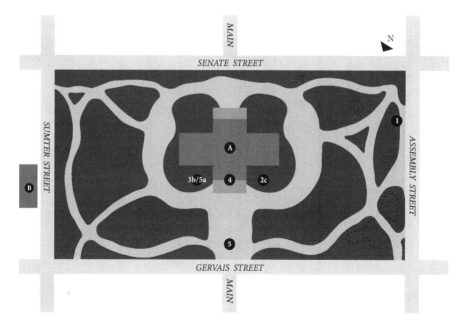

The South Carolina State House Grounds, 1878–1903

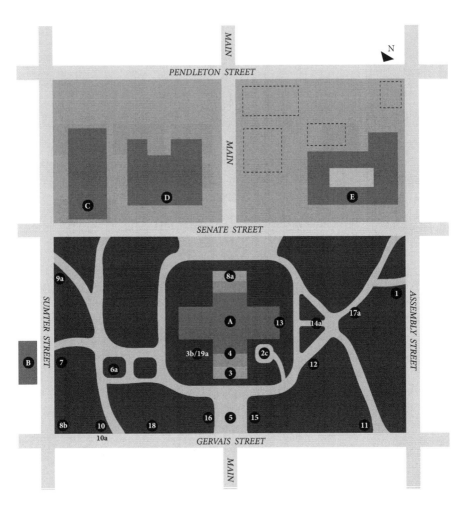

The South Carolina State House Grounds, 1903–68

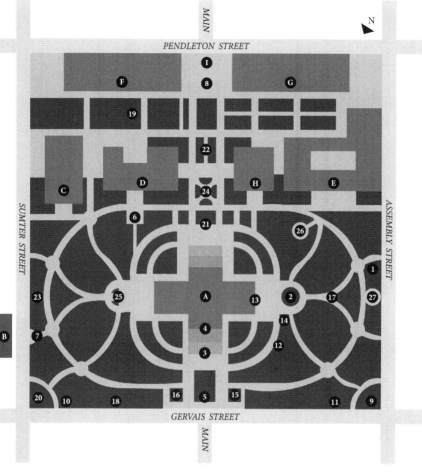

The South Carolina State House Grounds, 1969–present

Abbreviations Used in Notes

CR	*Columbia Record*
CS	*State* (Columbia)
HKB	Henry Kirke Brown
JGR	John Gardiner Richards Jr.
RCPL	Walker Local History Room, Richland County Public Library
REM	Robert E. Marvin
SCHJ	*Journal of the House of Representatives of the State of South Carolina*
SCSJ	*Journal of the Senate of the State of South Carolina*
SCDAH	South Carolina State Archives, South Carolina Department of Archives and History, Columbia
SoCar	South Caroliniana Library, University of South Carolina, Columbia

Notes

Introduction

1. William E. Hughes, "Gen. Hampton Rides Again," *CS*, October 16, 1969.
2. Mrs. Clark Waring quoted in "The Wade Hampton Chapter," *CS*, December 28, 1902.
3. On defining and studying cultural landscapes, see Chris Wilson and Paul Groth, eds., *Everyday America: Cultural Landscape Studies after J. B. Jackson* (Berkeley: University of California Press, 2003); and Richard Longstreth, ed., *Cultural Landscapes: Balancing Nature and Heritage in Preservation Practice* (University of Minnesota Press, 2008).
4. On this approach, see James W. Loewen, *Lies Across America: What Our Historic Sites and National Monuments Get Wrong* (New York: New Press, 1999).

One: Building and Challenging a Sovereign State House
South Carolina State House

1. The state's colonial legislature met in rented rooms from the colony's founding in 1670 until constructing its own building in Charleston 1753–70. The first capitol burned in 1788; a new one was built soon after and is still used as the Charleston County Courthouse. See A. S. Salley, *The State Houses of South Carolina, 1751–1936* (Columbia: Cary Printing Company, 1936), 1–7, 975.7711 Sa3s, SoCar.
2. The first Columbia State House has long been rumored to have been designed by James Hoban, the architect of the White House, but this is unlikely. See John M. Bryan, *Creating the South Carolina State House* (Columbia: University of South Carolina Press, 1999), 6–8.
3. Bryan, *Creading the South Carolina State House*, 10–13.
4. *Diary of Edward Hooker, 1805–1808* (Washington, DC: Government Printing Office, 1897), 854, Kohn-Henning Collection, SoCar.
5. Bryan, *Creating the South Carolina State House*, 10–17.

6. Whitemarsh Benjamin Seabrook, "Message of the Governor of South Carolina to the Legislature," November 27, 1850, repr. in *The Carolina Tribute to Calhoun*, ed. J. P. Thomas (Columbia: Richard L. Bryan, 1857), 330. Efforts to build a monument to Calhoun quickly shifted to Charleston. See Thomas J. Brown, *Civil War Canon: Sites of Confederate Memory in South Carolina* (Chapel Hill: University of North Carolina Press, 2015), 36–51.

7. Bryan, *Creating the South Carolina State House*, 10–17; Salley, *State Houses of South Carolina*, 9–16.

8. "The Capitol," *Camden Weekly Journal*, April 25, 1854.

9. John C. Calhoun, "On the Slavery Question, delivered in the Senate, March 4th, 1850," repr. in *Speeches of John C. Calhoun, Delivered in the House of Representatives and in the Senate of the United States*, ed. Richard K. Crallé (New York: D. Appleton & Company, 1883), 542–73.

10. *SCHJ* (1854), 18–20; Bryan, *Creating the South Carolina State House*, 17–24.

11. "Editorial Correspondence," *Camden Weekly Journal*, December 19, 1854.

12. *SCHJ* (1854), 20.

13. Bryan, *Creating the South Carolina State House*, 25–38.

14. "Laying the Corner-Stone," *Abbeville Press and Banner*, June 20, 1856.

15. Bryan, *Creating the South Carolina State House*, 35–46.

16. *Charleston Courier*, December 7, 1860. On the problems of the quarry, see Bryan, *Creating the South Carolina State House*, 45–47.

17. Bryan, *Creating the South Carolina State House*, 45.

18. Bryan, *Creating the South Carolina State House*, 56–59.

19. William Gilmore Simms, *A City Laid Waste: The Capture, Sack, and Destruction of the City of Columbia* (1865, repr. Columbia: University of South Carolina Press, 2005), 106.

20. "The State House of South Carolina," *Yorkville Enquirer*, August 23, 1866.

21. The Reconstruction legislature met in various places around Columbia (including the library at the University of South Carolina, now the South Caroliniana Library) until the November 1868 regular session. See *SCSJ* (1868), 3; and "From the State Capital," *Anderson Intelligencer*, November 25, 1869.

22. Charles Vincent, *Black Legislators in Louisiana During Reconstruction* (Carbondale: Southern Illinois University Press, 2011), 219.

23. Bryan, *Creating the South Carolina State House*, 92–96. For the history of convict labor in South Carolina after the Civil War, see Matthew J.

Mancini, *One Dies, Get Another: Convict Leasing in the American South, 1866–1928* (Columbia: University of South Carolina Press, 1996), 198–214.

24. Bryan, *Creating the South Carolina State House*, 93–102.
25. "The Capitol's Costly Interior," CS, May 28, 1891.
26. Bryan, *Creating the South Carolina State House*, 102–11.
27. *Orangeburg Times and Democrat*, January 10, 1900; Bryan, *Creating the South Carolina State House*, 113–15.
28. Daniel J. Vivian, "'A Practical Architect': Frank P. Milburn and the Transformation of Architectural Practice in the New South, 1890–1925," *Winterthur Portfolio* 40, no. 1 (Spring 2005): 17–28. Extant Milburn-designed buildings in Columbia include St. Peter's Church, the Union Passenger Station (now California Dreaming restaurant), and 1205 Pulaski Street (the South Carolina Dispensary Office Building). His City Hall stood across from the State House until it was demolished in 1938 for the Wade Hampton Hotel. See Frank P. Milburn, *Designs from the Work of Frank P. Milburn, Architect, Columbia, SC* (Columbia: State Printing Company, 1903).
29. This idea was originally introduced by local architect Gadsden E. Shand a few months before Milburn won the contract. See Bryan, *Creating the South Carolina State House*, 113–18. Milburn also added a dome to the Florida State Capitol in the same period as the South Carolina commission.
30. *SCHJ* (1905), 480; "The State House Dome and the Record," CS, June 27, 1904.
31. *Report of the Commission for Completion of State House* (Columbia: Gonzales and Bryan, 1907–8), 444.
32. Alexander Salley ended his history of the building: "And so the State House is still in many respects incomplete." Salley, *State Houses of South Carolina*, 39.

Swanson Lunsford Grave

33. Helen Kohn Hennig, "Lonely Grave on State House Grounds Holds Dust of Revolutionary Soldier, Captain under Light Horse Harry Lee," CS, March 21, 1936; *Acts of the General Assembly of the State of South-Carolina from December, 1795, to December, 1804, Both Inclusive* (Columbia: D. & J. J. Faust, 1808), 2:162, 222.
34. *Charleston City Gazette*, August 16, 1799; "The Lonely Grave on Capitol Square," CS, October 9, 1899.
35. Hennig, "Lonely Grave on State House Grounds"; "Revolutionary

Hero's Lone Grave on Capitol Grounds Is Cleared," *CR*, December 29, 1924. That Lunsford owned the land was one of the most persistent theories, later disproven by state historian Alexander Salley. See "Heroes's [*sic*] Grave," *Newberry Weekly Herald*, November 22, 1907.

36. This was state historian Alexander Salley's conclusion after a lifetime of research. See A. S. Salley, "There's a One-Grave Cemetery on the State House Grounds," *CS*, December 28, 1952; "State House and Grounds, Always Lovely, Alluring," *CS*, March 22, 1931; and Harlan Edwards, "Morning Stroll in Columbia," *CS*, September 3, 1938.

37. John Douglass, petition to the South Carolina Senate, ca. 1836, Item 00623, Petitions to the General Assembly, SCDAH.

38. See *Acts and Resolutions of the General Assembly of the State of South Carolina, passed in December 1836* (Columbia: S. Weir, State Printer, 1837), 116.

39. See Michael G. Kammen, *A Season of Youth: The American Revolution and the Historical Imagination* (New York: Knopf, 1978).

40. "The Lonely Grave on Capitol Square." See also *SCHJ* (1879), 133.

41. "Heroes's Grave"; "Swanson Lunsford's Grave," *CS*, December 6, 1907.

42. "Sons of Revolution Caring for Lone Grave of Patriot," *CS*, December 28, 1924; "Stone Removed by Relatives," *CS*, August 27, 1927. The work was completed by Bruns & Davis.

43. "State House Grave Gains Fresh Dignity," *CS*, June 5, 1953.

George Washington Monument

44. On Houdon and the Washington sculpture, see Anne L. Poulet, *Jean-Antoine Houdon: Sculptor of the Enlightenment* (Chicago: University of Chicago Press, 2005); and Maurie D. McInnis, "Revisiting Cincinnatus: Houdon's *George Washington*," in *Shaping the Body Politic: Art and Political Formation in Early America*, ed. McInnis and Louis P. Nelson (Charlottesville: University of Virginia Press, 2011), 128–61.

45. "Houdon's Statue," *Richmond Dispatch*, January 14, 1853. On Hubard, see Alexander G. Gilliam Jr., "Our Own Virginia Artist," *Virginia Cavalcade* (Autumn 1961): 10–19; and Albert Ten Eyck Gardner, "Southern Monuments: Charles Carroll and William James Hubard," *Metropolitan Museum of Art Bulletin*, new series, 17, no. 1 (Summer 1958): 19–23.

46. See Lauretta Dimmick, "'An Altar Erected to Heroic Virtue Itself': Thomas Crawford and His 'Virginia Washington Monument,'" *American Art Journal* 23, no. 2 (1991): 4–73.

47. "Houdon's Statue of Washington," *Southern Literary Messenger* 18, no. 10 (October 1852): v; *Richmond Daily Dispatch*, September 20, 1853. On Canova's Washington, see Xavier F. Salomon, Guido Beltramini, and Mario Guderzo, *Canova's George Washington* (New York: The Frick Collection, 2018).

48. *Richmond Daily Dispatch*, September 20, 1853.

49. HKB and the Ames Manufacturing Company in Chicopee, Massachusetts, cast the first bronze sculptures in the United States in the late 1840s. See Michael Edward Shapiro, *Bronze Casting and American Sculpture, 1850–1900* (Newark: University of Delaware Press, 1985), 34–60.

50. "Hubard's Washington," *Charleston Daily Courier*, June 16, 1858. The six copies are now located at the South Carolina and North Carolina State Houses, a St. Louis park, Virginia Military Institute, Miami University (originally sold to the University of Missouri after Hubard's death), and New York City (sold after Hubard's death).

51. W. J. Hubard, "Houdon's Statue in the Capitol," *Washington Sentinel*, April 1, 1854; "Houdon's Statue of Washington," *Lady's Home Magazine* 16 (November 1860): 316.

52. "Art," *New York Observer and Chronicle* 37, no. 2 (January 13, 1859): 14; "Houdon's Statue," *Richmond Dispatch*, March 18, 1854; *Richmond Daily Dispatch*, September 20, 1853.

53. "Explosion of a Bombshell," *Charleston Courier*, February 18, 1862; Gardner, "Southern Monuments."

54. "Washington Statue to be Erected Here," *Newport Mercury*, November 20, 1931. The Virginia legislature authorized the Gorham Company to produce the second wave of bronze copies in 1910.

55. Smithsonian American Art Museum, American Art Inventories Catalog, Control Number 760006401, available at https://americanart.si.edu/research/inventories. Senator Andrew Pickens Butler suggested the purchase to then-governor Robert Francis Withers Allston, likely after seeing Hubard's cast at the US Capitol. See Robert Stockton, "R. F. W. Allston: Planter Patron," in *Art in the Lives of South Carolinians, Nineteenth-Century Chapters*, book 1, ed. David Moltke-Hansen (Charleston: Carolina Art Association, 1978), RSa-7-8, SoCar.

56. "For the Courier," *Charleston Courier*, March 2, 1858.

57. See Drew Gilpin Faust, *The Creation of Confederate Nationalism: Ideology and Identity in the Civil War South* (Baton Rouge: Louisiana State University Press, 1988); and Lydia Mattice Brandt, "Re-Creating

Mount Vernon: The Virginia Building at the 1893 Chicago World's Columbian Exposition," *Winterthur Portfolio* 43, no. 1 (Spring 2009): 79–113. Davis's February 22, 1862, presidential inauguration in Richmond was his second. His first was on February 18, 1861, in Montgomery, Alabama.

58. "A History of a Statue," *Manning Times* (SC), May 1, 1889.

59. "A Great Piece of Art," *CS*, March 3, 1903; "Capitol Grounds Need Attention," *CS*, December 15, 1906; "Pedestal for First Citizen," *CR*, March 11, 1911.

60. A. S. Salley Jr., "The Houdon Statue of George Washington," *CS*, January 8, 1907. The rotunda interior was also discussed as a potential location for the statue. A bronzed plaster cast of Frederick Wellington Ruckstull's statue of John C. Calhoun now occupies this place of honor. "The Houdon Statue," *CR*, August 23, 1910.

61. Simms, *A City Laid Waste*, 48.

62. A. I. Robertson, "The Houdon Statue of George Washington," *CS*, November 26, 1906; Salley, "The Houdon Statue of George Washington."

63. Charles H. Lesser, *The Palmetto State's Memory: A History of the South Carolina Department of Archives & History, 1905–1960* (Columbia: South Carolina Department of Archives & History, 2009), 20.

64. A. S. Salley Jr., *Report of the Historical Commission of South Carolina to the General Assembly of South Carolina at the Regular Session of 1931*, 5, SoCar.

Sculpture on the North Façade of the State House

65. John R. Niernsee to HKB, April 2, 1859, transcribed in Henry K. Bush-Brown, ed., "Henry Kirke Brown: The Father of American Sculpture," 1270, unpublished manuscript, MSS 0561, folder 16, box 1, University of Delaware Library, Wilmington (the Library of Congress holds another copy). HKB could have received the commission thanks to one or both of the following recommendations: Thomas Ustick Walter, then the architect for the US Capitol, recommended Brown to Niernsee and/or Brown had also recently developed a friendship with Thomas Green Clemson, son-in-law to John C. Calhoun. See J. R. Niernsee to HKB, March 10, 1860, transcribed in Bush-Brown, "Henry Kirke Brown," 1285-B; Kirk Savage, *Standing Soldiers, Kneeling Slaves: Race, War and Monument in Nineteenth-Century America* (Princeton, NJ: Princeton University Press, 1997), 204; and Wayne Craven, *Sculpture in America* (New York: Thomas Y. Crowell Company, 1968), 154–55.

66. Kren Yvonne Lemmey, "Henry Kirke Brown and the Development of American Public Sculpture in New York City, 1846–1876" (PhD diss., City University of New York, 2005), 186–203. On the depiction of African Americans on the capitol, see Vivien Green Fryd, *Art and Empire: The Politics of Ethnicity in the United States Capitol, 1815–1860* (Athens: Ohio University Press, 2001), 200–208.

67. HKB to Mr. Maynard, April 22, 1859, transcribed in Bush-Brown, "Henry Kirke Brown," 1271.

68. *SCHJ* (1859), 23. For other examples of their memory in the period, see "The Fusion in New York," *Camden Weekly Journal*, October 9, 1860; "Editorial Inklings," *Yorkville Enquirer*, July 19, 1860; and "An Appeal to the South," *Yorkville Enquirer*, December 13, 1860.

69. I am grateful to Thomas Brown for alerting me to this comparison.

70. See Karen S. York, "American Portrait Cameo Cutting: An Alternate Apprenticeship in Relief Sculpture, 1830–1870" (PhD diss., Indiana University, 2004). These are perhaps the only known portrait cameos executed in marble by HKB. See ibid., 92.

71. With five-pointed stars, six arrows, and fruited olive branches, they are specifically adaptations of the reinterpretation of the seal from 1841. See US Department of State, Bureau of Public Affairs, "The Great Seal of the United States," July 2003, https://diplomacy.state.gov/exhibits-programs/the-great-seal/.

72. Brown had used Houdon's bust of Washington—produced as a study for the Virginia state capitol sculpture—as a model for his equestrian statue earlier that decade.

73. William Morris Davis, "Heroism in Art," transcribed in Bush-Brown, "Henry Kirke Brown," 1358; Bryan, *Creating the South Carolina State House*, 56.

74. The work was planned more than a year before Abraham Lincoln's election, South Carolina's secession, and the entrance of Kansas and West Virginia to the Union. Some had suggested placing fifteen stars on the Confederacy's flag by early 1861. See Raphael P. Thian, *Documentary History of the Flag and Seal of the Confederate States of America, 1861–'65* (Washington, DC: Adjutant General's Office, 1880). My thanks to John Coski and Evie Terrono for their consultation on this symbolism.

75. HKB to Henry D. Udall, May 1, 1860, transcribed in Bush-Brown, "Henry Kirke Brown," 1285D–1286.

76. Savage, *Standing Soldiers*, 31–51.

77. Davis, "Heroism in Art," 1367–71.

78. "The New State Capitol," *Abbeville Press and Banner*, March 23, 1860.
79. HKB to Morris Davis, August 7, 1861, 1347, and HKB to Morris Davis, July 14, 1861, 1344, both transcribed in Bush-Brown, "Henry Kirke Brown."
80. Savage, *Standing Soldiers*, 31–51.
81. W. M. Davis to HKB, transcribed in Bush-Brown, "Henry Kirke Brown," 1276.
82. R. W. Gibbs to HKB, May 13, 1861, transcribed in Bush-Brown, "Henry Kirke Brown," 1333.

Palmetto Monument

83. Walter Edgar, *South Carolina: A History* (Columbia: University of South Carolina Press, 1998), 340–1. See also Jack Allen Meyer, *South Carolina in the Mexican War: A History of the Palmetto Regiment of Volunteers, 1846–1917* (Columbia: South Carolina Department of Archives and History, 1996). The palmetto has appeared on the state flag since 1861 and was designated the state tree in 1939.
84. Committee Report, 1847, Series: S165005, Year: ND00, Item: 03098, SCDAH; Resolution to request the Governor to report on the plan for the erection of a Monument to the officers and Men of the Palmetto Regiment, December 17, 1847, Series: S165018, Year: 1847, Item: 00032, SCDAH, http://www.archivesindex.sc.gov/.
85. "Monument to the Palmetto Regiment," *Charleston Daily Courier*, December 18, 1848; *Edgefield Advertiser*, December 27, 1848.
86. "Monument to Col. P. M. Butler," *Edgefield Advertiser*, July 24, 1851; "Palmetto Monument," *Lancaster News*, June 9, 1852.
87. "Battle of Churubusco," *Edgefield Advertiser*, September 4, 1851.
88. *Charleston Daily Courier*, November 17, 1853.
89. "Editorial Correspondence," *Camden Weekly Journal*, December 19, 1854. For Werner's work on the State House, see "The New State House," *Camden Weekly Journal*, December 20, 1853; and Kelly Ann Ciociola, "'Werner Fecit': Christopher Werner and Nineteenth-Century Charleston Ironwork" (master's thesis, Clemson University and the College of Charleston, 2010), 53–55. Werner erected the sculpture in anticipation of the location of the new State House; he installed it months after the old State House was moved.
90. Ciociola, "'Werner Fecit,'" 59–123.
91. Ciociola, "'Werner Fecit,'" 38–41.
92. Resolution to Direct the Commissioners of the New State Capitol

to Purchase Christopher Werner's Cast Iron Representation of the Palmetto Tree, ca. 1856, Series: S165018, Year: ND00, Item: 00943, SCDAH, http://www.archivesindex.sc.gov/; "Special Columbia Correspondence," *Edgefield Advertiser*, December 10, 1856. For public comment, see "Another Palmetto Gone," *Sumter Banner*, September 27, 1854; "The Late Col. Pierce M. Butler," *Edgefield Advertiser*, November 23, 1853; and "Governor Butler," *Edgefield Advertiser*, February 28, 1855.

93. Christopher Werner, Petition Asking to Provide Additional Funds to Cover the Cost of Correcting Names and Making Improvements on the Monument Erected to the Dead of the Palmetto Regiment, ca. 1856, Series: S165015, Year: ND00, Item: 04437, SCDAH, http://www.archivesindex.sc.gov/; Bryan, *Creating the South Carolina State House*, 40–41.

94. "Information Wanted," *Orangeburg Times and Democrat*, February 29, 1888.

95. Photographic evidence suggests that the posts and arches were in place until the monument was moved in 1874. See photograph by Walter Blanchard, Identifier max1505, https://localhistory.richland library.com/digital/collection/p16817coll17/id/1162/rec/5.

96. "Hurricane in Columbia," *Orangeburg Times*, May 8, 1875; "South Carolina News," *Yorkville Enquirer*, April 10, 1884.

97. "Leaves Numbered," *CS*, March 15, 1939; "The Palmetto Monument," *CS*, August 3, 1941.

98. "Gossip with Our Exchanges," *Abbeville Press and Banner*, September 9, 1874.

99. "Registered Dots," *Columbia Daily Register*, April 12, 1878; Lenova Page, "Grounds at State House to Be Picturesque Mall," *CS*, November 26, 1972.

Two. Jim Crow and the State House Beautiful

1. "The Father of His Country," *Newberry Weekly Herald*, May 18, 1881.

Plans for the State House Landscape

2. Letter dated May 17, 1842, reprinted in the *Charleston Courier*, May 19, 1843; "Correspondence of the Courier," *Charleston Courier*, August 20, 1850.

3. "Correspondence of the Courier," *Charleston Courier*, August 20, 1850.

4. "Correspondence of the Courier," *Charleston Courier*, August 16, 1847, and August 20, 1850; "Columbia," *Charleston Courier*, June 14, 1853; Bryan, *Creating the South Carolina State House*, 39.

5. "Editorial Correspondence," *Camden Weekly Journal*, December 19, 1854.

6. *SCHJ* (1873), 89.

7. *SCHJ* (1868/70), 217.

8. "Registered Dots," *Columbia Daily Register*, March 16, 1878. Schwagerl was paid $100 for the plans, a tidy sum for the cash-strapped government.

9. See David D. Rash, "Edward Otto Schwagerl," in *Shaping Seattle Architecture: A Historical Guide to the Architects*, ed. Jeffrey Karl Ochsner and Wayne P. Suttles, 2nd ed. (Seattle: University of Washington Press, 2014), 116–22. My thanks to David Hammack, Case Western Reserve University, for information on Schwagerl.

10. The drawing is unsigned but could be Schwagerl's "working drawing" paid for by the state or at the very least could be based on his design. The other two drawings (now presumed lost) were for "planting, and the third to show the grounds as they will be when the other plans are carried out." See Folder 5, map box 20, SCDAH; and "Returned Home," *Columbia Daily Register*, March 21, 1878.

11. "Registered Dots," *Columbia Daily Register*, April 7, 1878; R. M. Sims, "Report of the Secretary of State to the General Assembly of South Carolina," November 25, 1878, in *Reports and Resolutions to the General Assembly of the State of South Carolina, at the Regular Session of 1878* (Columbia: Calvo & Patton, State Printers, 1878), 387.

12. "Brevities," *Columbia Daily Register*, March 30, 1879; "Registered Dots," *Columbia Daily Register*, February 4, 1879.

13. "Judge Mackey's Return," *Pickens Sentinel*, April 4, 1877.

14. See Alan T. Nolan, "The Anatomy of the Myth," in *The Myth of the Lost Cause and Civil War History*, ed. Gary W. Gallagher and Alan T. Nolan (Bloomington: Indiana University Press, 2000).

15. For other examples, see Louis P. Nelson, "Monuments and Memory in Charlottesville," *Buildings & Landscapes* 25, no. 2 (Fall 2018): 17–35; and Catherine Bishir, "Landmarks of Power: Building a Southern Past, 1885-1915," in *Southern Built: American Architecture, Regional Practice* (Charlottesville: University of Virginia Press, 2006), 254–93.

16. "The Coming of Spring in a Great Metropolis," *CS*, May 6, 1900.

17. "Why Not 'a City Beautiful?'" *CS*, December 31, 1903.

18. See Jon A. Peterson, *The Birth of City Planning in the United States, 1840–1917* (Baltimore: Johns Hopkins University Press, 2003).

19. On Harlan P. Kelsey's plans for Greenville and Columbia, SC, see Marta Leslie Thacker, "Working for the City Beautiful: Civic Improvement in Three South Carolina Communities" (master's thesis, University of South Carolina, 1990).

20. Kelsey & Guild, *The Improvement of Columbia South Carolina; Report to the Civic League, Columbia, South Carolina* (Harrisburg, Pa.: Mount Pleasant Press, 1905).

21. Kelsey & Guild, *The Improvement of Columbia,* 16–19, 64.

22. Kelsey & Guild, *The Improvement of Columbia,* 19.

23. The original spelling of Ruckstull's name was "Ruckstuhl." The artist changed it in 1918 to sound less German in the wake of World War I. See "Ruckstull Changes Spelling of Name," *CS*, January 20, 1918.

24. F. Wellington Ruckstuhl, *The Value of Beauty to a City* (Columbia: The State Company for the Civic Improvement League, Columbia, 1905), 12.

25. His bronzed plaster copy of the Calhoun statue stands in the State House lobby today.

26. "An Appeal to the Women," *CS*, October 29, 1906.

27. *Report of the Secretary of State to the General Assembly of South Carolina,* part 1 (Columbia: Gonzaels and Bryan, 1907–8), 56–57.

28. *SCHJ* (1907), 92.

29. "Seen Here and There," *CS*, July 19, 1960.

30. *SCHJ* (1903), 408.

31. "Put Them Underground," *CS*, February 2, 1967.

South Carolina Monument to the Confederate Dead
(Confederate Monument)

32. See Caroline E. Janney, *Burying the Dead but Not the Past: Ladies' Memorial Associations and the Lost Cause* (Chapel Hill: University of North Carolina Press, 2008), 69–103.

33. Brown, *Civil War Canon,* 93–94.

34. "A Grand Day in Columbia," *Newberry Weekly Herald,* May 21, 1879.

35. "Cost of the Monument," *Abbeville Press and Banner,* May 21, 1879.

36. "Cost of the Monument."

37. Michael Wilson Panhorst, "Lest We Forget: Monuments and Memorial Sculpture in National Military Parks on Civil War Battlefields,

1861–1917" (PhD diss., University of Delaware, 1988), 210–32; Brown, *Civil War Canon*, 93–106.

38. Savage, *Standing Soldiers, Kneeling Slaves*, 162–208.

39. Brown, *Civil War Canon*, 98.

40. "South Carolina News," *Yorkville Enquirer*, April 3, 1879; "Unveiling the Monument," *Anderson Intelligencer*, May 22, 1879.

41. "The Confederate Monument on the Capitol Grounds," CS, February 5, 1905.

42. "Love's Labor Lost," *Anderson Intelligencer*, June 29, 1882.

Wade Hampton Monument

43. See Rod Andrew Jr., *Wade Hampton: Confederate Warrior to Southern Redeemer* (Chapel Hill: University of North Carolina Press, 2008); and Bruce E. Baker, *What Reconstruction Meant: Historical Memory in the American South* (Charlottesville: University of Virginia Press, 2007).

44. "Movement Started for the Monument," CS, April 17, 1902; "Hampton Monument Commission," CS, April 2, 1903.

45. "Need Money for Hampton Statue," CS, December 10, 1903; "Hampton Statue Will Be Erected," CS, February 26, 1904.

46. *SCHJ* (1903), 168–69.

47. "Hampton Monument Bill Passes House," CS, February 13, 1903; "Ruckstall [*sic*] to Model Statue of Hampton," CS, June 16, 1904.

48. "Ruckstuhl's Conception of the Hampton Monument," CS, November 20, 1906.

49. "To Make a Sketch of Hampton Statue," CS, October 19, 1904; "Would Like Monument Placed at Postoffice," CS, May 14, 1905.

50. "Ruckstuhl's Model Has Been Accepted," CS, November 29, 1904.

51. Ruckstuhl, *The Value of Beauty to a City*, 10; "Ruckstuhl's Model Has Been Accepted."

52. "To Make a Sketch of Hampton Statue"; "Sepulcher of Wade Hampton," CS, March 20, 1904. The state's appropriation specified that the statue must be placed on the State House grounds.

53. "Orders Issued for the Parade," CS, November 19, 1906; "Statue of Hampton Given to the State," CS, November 21, 1906.

54. *Anderson Intelligencer*, reprinted in "Hampton Monument," CS, November 27, 1906.

55. "Our Mutilated Monuments a Disgrace," CS, August 23, 1927.

56. "Noted Sculptor Visits Columbia," CS, March 29, 1931; "Reletter Legend Hampton Statue," CS, July 21, 1931.

57. "The State House," *CS*, October 1, 1969.

Partisan Generals Monument

58. See Walter Edgar, *Partisans and Redcoats: The Southern Conflict that Turned the Tide of the American Revolution* (New York: HarperCollins, 2001).

59. "Memorial Honors for Partisan Generals Will Unveil," *CS*, November 9, 1913.

60. "Monument to the Three Partizan [*sic*] Leaders," *CS*, December 24, 1906; *Reports and Resolutions of the General Assembly of the State of South Carolina, Regular Session Commencing January 13, 1914*, vol. 4 (Columbia: Gonzales and Bryan, State Printers, 1913–14), 502; "Memorial Honors for Partisan Generals Will Unveil."

61. "With the Daughters of the Revolution," *CS*, October 30, 1902. The column's estimated value was $1,200.

62. "Memorial Honors for Partisan Generals Will Unveil." On Robertson, see "Columbia Artist Has Passed Away," *CS*, January 8, 1913.

63. "Monument Plans Are Accepted," *CS*, January 6, 1909; "Memorial Honors for Partisan Generals Will Unveil."

64. "Monument Be Best of Kind in This Land," *CR*, October 12, 1912; "Monument to be Unveiled Nov. 11," *CR*, October 16, 1913; "Memorial Shaft Erection Begun," *CS*, October 24, 1913. Conflicting reports make it difficult to determine the source for the various granites used in the monument.

65. "Ruckstuhl Shows Monument Plans," *CS*, October 10, 1912.

66. "State Convention of the D.A.R. in Columbia Today," *CR*, November 12, 1913.

67. See Virginia Mason Bratton, *History of the South Carolina Daughters of the American Revolution, 1892–1936* (South Carolina Daughters of the American Revolution, 1937), 13–17; and "Tribute Is Paid Late Mrs. Bacon," *CR*, January 7, 1916. On the overlap between women's club membership and racism, see Joan Marie Johnson, "'As Intensely Southern As I Am': Black and White Clubwomen, the United Daughters of the Confederacy, and Southern Identity," in *Southern Ladies, New Women: Race, Region, and Clubwomen in South Carolina, 1890–1930* (Gainesville: University Press of Florida, 2004), 24–59.

68. "Leaders' Names Will Echo Down the Halls of Time," *CS*, November 12, 1913.

Monument to the Women of the Confederacy
(Confederate Women's Monument)

69. Broadus Mitchell, "Ruckstuhl on His Work," *CR*, January 1, 1912.
70. See Zachary Lynn Elledge, "Defeat and Memory at the Arkansas State Capitol: The Little Rock Monument to the Women of the Confederacy" (master's thesis, Arkansas State University, 2015); Thomas J. Brown, "The Confederate Retreat to Mars and Venus," in *Battle Scars: Gender and Sexuality in the American Civil War*, ed. Catherine Clinton and Nina Sibler (Oxford: Oxford University Press, 2006), 189–213; and Brown, *Civil War Canon*, 112–25.
71. Elledge, "Defeat and Memory at the Arkansas State Capitol," 29–31.
72. *SCHJ* (1900), 396. Others were built in Raleigh, North Carolina (1914); Little Rock, Arkansas (1913); Jacksonville, Florida (1915); Jackson, Mississippi (1917); Baltimore, Maryland (1917, removed 2017); Nashville, Tennessee (1926).
73. "How the Fund Grew in the State's Care," *CS*, April 12, 1912.
74. Broadus Mitchell, "Ruckstuhl on His Work," *CR*, January 1, 1912.
75. "South Carolinians Join to Honor Heroic Women of the Confederacy," *CS*, April 12, 1912.
76. "Monument Site Most Pleasing," *CS*, April 13, 1912.
77. "Our Mutilated Monuments a Disgrace," *CS*, August 23, 1927; "Contract Let Move Monument," *CS*, August 23, 1935.
78. State House Speech, "State Capital Grounds Update 880810" folder, box 75, REM Landscape Architectural Collection, SoCar.

Spanish-American War Monuments

79. See Harris Moore Bailey Jr., "The Splendid Little Forgotten War: The Mobilization of South Carolina for the War with Spain," *The South Carolina Historical Magazine* 92, no. 3 (July 1991): 189–214; and Edgar, *South Carolina: A History*, 466.
80. See Nina Sibler, *The Romance of Reunion: Northerners and the South, 1865–1900* (Chapel Hill: University of North Carolina Press, 1993), 178–85.
81. "That Spanish Cannon," *CS*, January 31, 1900; Cheves Ligon, "Old Field Pieces Rusting Away on Capitol Grounds," *CR*, August 25, 1942.
82. For examples, see Charles Shabica, "Admiral Dewey's Cannon," Winnetka Historical Society blog, n.d., http://www.winnetkahistory.org/gazette/admiral-deweys-cannon/; and "Forest Park Statues and

Monuments," n.d., http://www.forestparkstatues.org/spanish-cannon -examinador/.

83. City Council Minutes of Columbia, South Carolina, August 21, 1900 and September 11, 1900, South Carolina Digital Library, http:// digital.tcl.sc.edu/cdm/search/collection/citymin.

84. "'Spanish' Cannon Added to Scrap," *CS*, October 17, 1942.

85. Ligon, "Old Field Pieces Rusting Away on Capitol Grounds"; R. E. Grier, "Around the State House," *CS*, October 10, 1942; "City Hall Bell, Spanish War Cannon Off to War," *CS*, October 18, 1942.

86. "An Incidental Benefit," *CS*, July 8, 1941.

87. Carl A. Zimring, *Cash for Your Trash: Scrap Recycling in America* (New Brunswick, NJ: Rutgers University Press, 2005), 94.

88. "City Accepts Six Pounder from *Maine*," *CR*, June 2, 1913.

89. "New Ornaments at Irwin Park," *CR*, December 12, 1914; David Charles McQuillan, "The Street Railway and the Growth of Columbia, South Carolina, 1882–1936" (master's thesis, University of South Carolina, 1975), 25.

90. "Want Maine's Gun Moved to Capitol," *CR*, March 11, 1928. On the demise of Irwin Park, see John Hammond Moore, *Columbia and Richland County: A South Carolina Community, 1740–1990* (Columbia: University of South Carolina Press, 1993), 317.

91. "Will Unveil Gun during Fair Week," *CS*, October 5, 1931.

92. "Spanish-Veterans Gather Thursday," *CS*, October 21, 1931.

93. "Spanish War Gun Dedicated Here," *CR*, October 23, 1931; "Gun Recalls Stirring Days of Spanish War," *CS*, October 23, 1931.

94. "Spanish War Veterans and Auxiliary Have Barbeque and Picnic," *CS*, July 9, 1936. The veteran's group was named after the Sumter-born chief engineer of the Panama Canal, David DuBose Gaillard.

95. "Spanish War Veterans to Meet in Columbia Thursday Night," *CS*, October 18, 1936.

96. "Monument," *CS*, May 12, 1941; "To Aid Monument," *CS*, September 13, 1941.

97. "Spanish War Veterans Unveil Monument at State House," *CS*, October 23, 1941.

98. "Monument," *CS*, May 12, 1941.

99. "To Aid Monument."

100. On Kitson, see Sarah Denver Beetham, "Sculpting the Citizen Soldier: Reproduction and National Memory, 1865–1917" (PhD diss., University of Delaware, 2014), 273–80.

101. Beetham, "Sculpting the Citizen Soldier," 46–138.

James Marion Sims Monument

102. "State Press," *CS*, July 28, 1907; Ethel G. Blatt, "Mrs. Stuckey Describes Long Campaign Culminating in Memorial to Surgeon," *CS*, May 10, 1929.

103. "The Sims Statue Unveiled," *New York Times*, October 21, 1894; "The Elderly Visitor," *CS*, September 4, 1910.

104. Deirdre Cooper Owens, *Medical Bondage: Race, Gender, and the Origins of American Gynecology* (Athens: University of Georgia Press, 2017).

105. J. Marion Sims, *The Story of My Life* (New York: D. Appleton and Company, 1884); Owens, *Medical Bondage*.

106. "Prohibition Discussion Is Deferred," *CR*, January 27, 1910.

107. "Memorial to Marion Sims," *CR*, February 15, 1912; "Will Pay Tribute to Noted Surgeon," *CS*, February 20, 1912. As with the Hampton Monument, the state appropriation was initially contingent upon private donations for half of the project's budget.

108. "Raise Monument to Marion Sims," *CS*, April 19, 1912.

109. "Women of State Would Honor James Marion Sims, World-Honored," *CR*, December 4, 1927; Blatt, "Mrs. Stuckey Describes Long Campaign."

110. "Sims Memorial Cost $6,265," *CR*, May 14, 1929.

111. "Famous Surgeon, South Carolinian, Will Be Honored," *CR*, May 5, 1929; Blatt, "Mrs. Stuckey Describes Long Campaign."

112. Blatt, "Mrs. Stuckey Describes Long Campaign."

113. R. E. Grier, "Around the State House," *CS*, October 25, 1941; "Monument Defaced," *CR*, February 9, 1946. Like the Hampton Monument, the Sims Monument's text was originally bronze and was later engraved. See "Sims Monument to Be Repaired," *CS*, February 8, 1936.

114. "The State House: Statue to Be Moved," *CS*, October 1, 1969.

115. See "Women of State Would Honor James Marion Sims."

116. Mayoral Advisory Commission on City Art, Monuments, and Markers, "Report to the City of New York, January 2018," 21, https://www1.nyc.gov/assets/monuments/downloads/pdf/mac-monuments-report.pdf. The monument was moved to Sims's grave in Green-Wood Cemetery; Nicole Brown, "J. Marion Sims statue in Central Park Moved to Green-Wood Cemetery," *AM New York*, April 17, 2018, https://www.amny.com/news/j-marion-sims-statue-1.18108650.

Jefferson Davis and Robert E. Lee
Memorial Highway Markers

117. On the UDC, see Karen L. Cox, *Dixie's Daughters: The United Daughters of the Confederacy and the Preservation of Confederate Culture* (Gainesville: University Press of Florida, 2003). On the UDC in South Carolina, see Joan Marie Johnson, *Southern Ladies, New Women: Race, Region, and Clubwomen in South Carolina, 1890–1930* (Gainesville: University Press of Florida, 2004); Eloise Welch Wright, "A Short History of the South Carolina Division, United Daughters of the Confederacy," part 1 (December 5, 1917), SoCar; and Mary B. Poppenheim et al., *The History of the United Daughters of the Confederacy,* vol. 1 (Raleigh, NC: Edwards and Broughton, 1956; repr. 1988).

118. See Gary W. Gallagher, *Lee and His Generals in War and Memory* (Baton Rouge: Louisiana State University Press, 1988); and Donald E. Collins, *The Death and Resurrection of Jefferson Davis* (Lanham, MD: Rowman & Littlefield, 2005).

119. Poppenheim et al., *History of the UDC,* 80, 86.

120. Richard F. Weingroff, "Jefferson Davis Memorial Highway," US Department of Transportation, Federal Highway Administration, updated June 27, 2017, https://www.fhwa.dot.gov/infrastructure/jdavis.cfm; Euan Hague and Edward H. Sebesta, "The Jefferson Davis Highway: Contesting the Confederacy in the Pacific Northwest," *Journal of American Studies* 45, no. 2 (May 2011): 289–91.

121. Wright, "A Short History of the South Carolina Division," 2. A map of the route appears in United Daughters of the Confederacy, South Carolina Division, "Jefferson Davis National Highway through South Carolina," pamphlet, 917.57Un3j, SoCar.

122. Cox, *Dixie's Daughters,* 64–65.

123. "Bridge Tournament," *CS,* June 17, 1923. On the standard marker, see Poppenheim et al., *History of the UDC,* 85.

124. "Daughters Give Boulder to City," *CS,* November 2, 1923.

125. "A Girl of the '60s Speaks," *CS,* November 18, 1923; "Gervais Is No. 1 Columbia Paving Project," *CS,* August 9, 1946; "Gervais Street Widening Is 30 Days Ahead of Schedule," *CS,* December 15, 1949. The marker was in place on Gervais Street by 1952. "Seen Here and There," *CS,* November 8, 1952.

126. Howard Lawrence Preston, *Dirt Roads to Dixie: Accessibility and Modernization in the South, 1885–1935* (Knoxville: University of Tennessee

Press, 1991), 128–32. See also Hague and Sebesta, "The Jefferson Davis Highway," 281–301; Weingroff, "Jefferson Davis Memorial Highway."

127. "Marker Moved in Gervais Street Widening," *CR*, November 28, 1962.

128. "Attend Unveiling of Marker in Charleston," *CS*, May 25, 1948.

129. "House Votes Confidence in Speaker Sol Blatt," *CS*, March 11, 1938; "Local Measures Ready to Sign," *CS*, May 7, 1938; R. E. Grier, "Around the State House," *CS*, May 7, 1938.

130. "Economic Development History of Interstate 26 in South Carolina," US Department of Transportation, Federal Highway Administration, https://www.fhwa.dot.gov/planning/economic_development/studies/i26sc.cfm.

131. On the reunion, see "Program Given for Rally of Confederates," *CR*, August 15, 1938.

132. "Living Confederate Flag Formed This Afternoon," *CS*, August 30, 1938. See also Cox, *Dixie's Daughters*, 64–65.

133. "Memorial Tree and Highway Marker Dedicated by UDC," *CS*, August 31, 1938.

Memorial Trees on the State House Grounds

134. Kirk Savage, *Monument Wars: Washington, D.C., the National Mall, and the Transformation of the Memorial Landscape* (Berkeley: University of California Press, 2005), 92–94.

135. Lydia Mattice Brandt, *First in the Homes of His Countrymen: George Washington's Mount Vernon in the American Imagination* (Charlottesville: University of Virginia Press, 2016), 131–32.

136. "The Cambridge Washington Elm," *Bulletin of Popular Information*, Arnold Arboretum, Harvard University 5, no. 18 (December 10, 1931), 69–73, http://arnoldia.arboretum.harvard.edu/pdf/articles/1931-5--the-cambridge-washington-elm.pdf.

137. "Parade Marks Elm Planting," *CR*, March 17, 1932.

138. "Washington Elm to Be Dedicated Here Friday," *CS*, September 1, 1947.

139. "Revolutionary War Elm Tree Dedicated to State as Aid to Combat Foreign Ideologies," *CS*, September 6, 1947.

140. "Historic Tree Set on Capitol Lawn," *CS*, March 20, 1932.

141. "That All Who Pause Might Know That Tree Keeps Green a Memory," *CS*, April 14, 1935; Thomas McMahan, "Capitol Capsules," *CR*, December 12, 1962.

142. "Tentative Plans Made for Dedication, Pageant during Confederate Reunion," *CS*, August 7, 1938.

143. "Parent-Teachers Open New Session," *CS*, November 19, 1930.

144. "Historic Spades and Flag to Be Used at Tree Planting Exercises," *CS*, March 17, 1932; "Historic Tree Set on Capitol Lawn," *CS*, March 20, 1932; "Constitution Is DAR Topic," *CR*, September 12, 1968.

145. "The Cork Tree," postcard, rich.cc.21c.2, AEY1244, Historic Columbia Collection; Elizabeth White, "History and Beauty Dignify State House Grounds," *CR*, October 3, 1967.

146. Patricia McNeely, "Bored on the 4th? Look for a Tree," *CR*, July 4, 1967.

John C. Calhoun State Office Building

147. "City Councilman Questions Tie Bids," *CR*, September 3, 1969.

148. "Six Ballots See Lines Holding in Judge Race," *CS*, February 15, 1940.

149. "Gov. Heyward's Message to the General Assembly," *CS*, January 9, 1907.

150. *Report of the Joint Committee on Economy and Consolidation, Appointed by the General Assembly Session of 1921, Submitted to the Regular Session of 1922* (Columbia: Gonzales and Bryan, State Printers, 1922), 74–75; Lydia Mattice Brandt, "Union National Bank Building," National Register of Historic Places Nomination Form, passed August 2018.

151. "House Approves Office Building," *CS*, February 20, 1924; "Office Building Now Guaranteed," *CS*, March 1, 1924.

152. "Tatum Selected by Commission," *CS*, April 22, 1924; Harold Tatum, "Questionnaire for Architects' Roster and/or Register of Architects Qualified for Federal Public Works," May 8, 1946, AIA Archives, http://content.aia.org/sites/default/files/2018-09/TatumHarold_roster.pdf; Anjuli Grantham, "John C. Calhoun State Office Building," National Register of Historic Places Nomination Form, passed 2011.

153. "In Two Bites," *CR*, March 23, 1926.

154. "State Office Building to Be a Thing of Beauty," *CS*, November 16, 1924.

155. "Needs More Money to Erect Building," *CS*, January 23, 1925; "Office Building Bill Gets New Lease on Life," *CS*, February 11, 1925; "Eight Hundred Thousand Require to Meet Cost," *CS*, March 26, 1925; "Three Million Dollar Program of Building On," *CR*, June 23, 1925.

156. "In Two Bites."

157. "Supreme Court May Get Its Own Building," *CR*, October 6, 1938.

158. Mayer Rus, "John C. Calhoun Building," *Interior Design* (November 1989): 190–93, "Calhoun Building" hanging file, RCPL.

Wade Hampton State Office Building

159. The state also built the War Memorial Building, a monument to the state's White World War I dead and administrative home for the SC Historical Commission, with funding from the Public Works Administration in 1935. The commission occupied the building until moving to a new purpose-built archive building on Senate Street in 1960, and the War Memorial is now part of the University of South Carolina campus. See Lesser, *The Palmetto State's Memory*.

160. "SC Government Outgrows Home; Needs Quarters," *CR*, June 22, 1936.

161. "Group Favors Building Site," *CR*, May 14, 1938; "Architects Bid to Conference," *CR*, October 11, 1938; "$54,000 Paid on State's Old Office Building," *CR*, June 14, 1939.

162. Christopher T. Ziegler, "Wade Hampton State Office Building," National Register of Historic Places Nomination Form, passed 2007.

Stars on the State House and
the Marker for the First State House

163. See Marion Brunson Lucas, *Sherman and the Burning of Columbia* (Columbia: University of South Carolina Press, repr. 2000).

164. After leaving its Senate Street building in the 2000s, the South Carolina Department of Archives and History moved state records to a facility off Farrow Road.

165. Lesser, *The Palmetto State's Memory*, 20; correspondence between Ruckstull and Salley in "Ruckstull, F. W." folder, RG: 108000, Series: 108066, SCDAH.

166. See Thomas J. Brown, "Monuments and Ruins: Atlanta and Columbia Remember Sherman," *Journal of American Studies* 51, no. 2 (May 2017): 411–36.

167. See A. S. Salley, "State Houses of South Carolina—1751 to Present," *CS*, March 21, 1936; and Brown, "Monuments and Ruins," 12–13. The rush of markers in the 1930s might also have been part of Salley's attempt to make his work more visible to the legislature, to increase his budget, and to ensure a new facility for the state's records.

168. "Sherman Shells' Scars on Capitol Are to Be Marked," *CR*, December 12, 1928.

169. "'Honorable Scars,'" *CR*, February 21, 1929; "Brass Stars Mark Spots Where Sherman Shells Hit," *CS*, March 29, 1929.

170. "Sherman Shells' Scars on Capitol Are to Be Marked." On "honorable scars," see Frances M. Clarke, *War Stories: Suffering and Sacrifice in the Civil War North* (Chicago: University of Chicago Press, 2011).
171. "Markers on Capitol Moved to Prevent Imminent Theft," *CS*, April 4, 1936.
172. R. E. Grier, "Around the State House," *CS*, May 11, 1937.
173. Salley, *The State Houses of South Carolina*, 39.
174. "Clemson Seeks Forestry Chair," *CS*, February 2, 1938; "Marker on Site Old State House," *CS*, February 25, 1938.

Benjamin Ryan Tillman Monument

175. "Byrnes Terms Ben Tillman 'The First New Dealer,'" *CS*, May 2, 1940.
176. Stephen Kantrowitz, *Ben Tillman & the Reconstruction of White Supremacy* (Chapel Hill: University of North Carolina Press, 2000); Edgar, *South Carolina: A History*, 430–52.
177. "Wants Monument to Ben Tillman," *CS*, June 9, 1929.
178. See J. G. Richards to Colonel W. W. Ball, May 12, 1939, folder 457, box 6, JGR Papers, SoCar.
179. *SCSJ* (1931), 20; Richards to Ball, May 12, 1939; "Tillman Drive Is Progressing," *CR*, April 24, 1937. As with the Hampton and Sims Monuments, the state appropriation was initially contingent upon private donations for half of the project's budget.
180. "Work to Begin on Monument to Ben Tillman," *CR*, May 10, 1939.
181. Minutes of the Meeting of the Tillman Memorial Commission, July 27, 1939, folder 457, box 6, JGR Papers, SoCar.
182. "Byrnes Terms Ben Tillman."
183. "Wants Monument to Ben Tillman."
184. Frances B. Simkins, "Benjamin Ryan Tillman," booklet printed for the Tillman Monument Commission, box 6, JGR Papers, SoCar. See also "Wants Monument to Ben Tillman"; "Byrnes Terms Ben Tillman."
185. Jack Irby Hayes Jr., *South Carolina and the New Deal* (Columbia: University of South Carolina Press, 2001), 158–75.

Liberty Bell Replica

186. "Bell . . ." *CS*, June 23, 1950. For the current locations and histories of the other replicas, see tomlovesthelibertybell.com.
187. Gary B. Nash, *The Liberty Bell* (New Haven: Yale University Press, 2010).
188. Nash, *The Liberty Bell*, 135–56.

189. Charlene Mires, *Independence Hall in American Memory* (Philadelphia: University of Pennsylvania Press, 2002), 236–38.

190. "Text of Truman Address at Liberty Bell Ceremony," *New York Times*, November 7, 1950.

191. "Liberty Bell Replica Is Presented to SC," *CR*, July 4, 1950; "Arsenal Hill Center Dance to Pay Tribute to Liberty Bell Drive," *CS*, June 6, 1950.

192. "State House Ornaments," *CS*, November 2, 1950.

193. Levona Page, "Grounds at State House to Be Picturesque Mall," *CS*, November 26, 1972; "Series E. Savings Bonds Anniversary Celebrated," *CS*, May 2, 1961; "Calendar," *CS*, May 1, 1991; "Events," *CS*, June 29, 2006.

Confederate Battle Flag

194. See John M. Coski, *The Confederate Battle Flag: America's Most Embattled Emblem* (Cambridge, Mass.: Belknap Press of Harvard University Press, 2005), 236–71. Mississippi's state flag incorporated the Confederate flag until 2020.

195. K. Michael Prince, *Rally 'Round the Flag, Boys! South Carolina and the Confederate Flag* (Columbia: University of South Carolina Press, 2004), 23–49.

196. "The 'Stars and Bars' Fly Again," *CS*, April 8, 1961; "Stars and Bars Are Now Waving Over the Capitol," *CS*, April 5, 1962.

197. Coski, *The Confederate Battle Flag*, 245.

198. Prince, *Rally 'Round the Flag, Boys!*, 195–247. Only three of the twenty-six Black representatives voted for the bill.

199. South Carolina Code of Laws, Title 10, Public Buildings and Property, sec. 10-1-165, "Protection of Certain Monuments and Memorials," https://www.scstatehouse.gov/code/t10c001.php; *SCHJ* (1999–2000).

200. Eugene Scott, "Nikki Haley: Confederate Flag 'Should Have Never Been There,'" *CNN*, July 10, 2015, https://www.cnn.com/2015/07/10/politics/nikki-haley-confederate-flag-removal/index.html. Haley later retreated from this position.

Three. Building for Bureaucracy

1. Levona Page, "Boom Puts SC in Space Race," *CS*, July 16, 1967.

James Francis Byrnes Monument

2. "Clark Dedicates Statue of Byrnes," *CR*, May 2, 1972; "Summer Repeat Series Premieres," *CS*, May 2, 1972.

3. Both Byrnes and his wife approved the sculpture during the planning process. See J. Bratton Davis to Charles C. Parks, July 11, 1969, author's collection.

4. See David Robertson, *Sly and Able: A Political Biography of James F. Byrnes* (New York: Norton, 1994), 492–548.

5. John Richard Craft to J. Bratton Davis, June 21, 1969, author's collection.

6. "The Byrnes Statue," *CR*, May 2, 1972; Cliff Harper to J. Bratton Davis, July 31, 1963, author's collection. Parks likely came at the recommendation of then-director of the Columbia Museum of Art, John Richard Craft.

7. John C. West to James H. Hammond, July 29, 1969, author's collection.

8. Justin Curry Davis, "Funding South Carolina's Monuments: The Growth of Corporate Person in Monument Financing" (master's thesis, University of South Carolina, 2017), 47. Thanks to Thomas Brown for bringing this to my attention.

9. James H. Hammond to John C. West, June 20, 1969, author's collection; "High Court Begins Move to Building," *CS*, January 19, 1971. The Monument to the Women of the Confederacy was then located in the corner site but was already slated to move as part of the reconfiguration of the grounds. See James H. Hammond to J. Bratton Davis, August 14, 1969, author's collection.

10. Charles C. Parks to REM, June 27, 1969, "Governor Byrnes' Statue Location" folder, box 8, REM Landscape Architectural Collection, SoCar.

11. The screen was to be up to fourteen feet tall and fifteen feet wide. See REM to John C. West et al., Memorandum, April 23, 1969, author's collection.

12. Charles C. Parks to John Bratton Davis, September 4, 1969, author's collection; Charles C. Parks to REM, June 27, 1969.

13. John Richard Craft to J. Bratton Davis, June 21, 1969, author's collection.

14. The capsule is to be opened on May 2, 2022. See "Dear Governor 2022," *CR*, January 13, 1975; and Charles C. Parks to N. Heyward Clarkson,

February 27, 1970, "Governor Byrnes' Statue Location" folder, box 8, REM Landscape Architectural Collection, SoCar.

15. March 1972 resolution quoted in "James F. Byrnes Day," May 2, 1972, pamphlet, author's collection.

Redesign of the State House Grounds

16. Mont Morton, "Sumter Legislator Offers Plans to Beautify State House's Front Grounds with Lagoons," *CS*, May 23, 1963.

17. "Grand Entrance for State House," *CR*, May 29, 1963.

18. Karen Patterson, "Crowd Generates Enthusiasm as Nixon Pays Columbia Visit," *CR*, November 3, 1960; Robert McHugh, "Johnson Blasts GOP 'Brinksmanship' in Major Appeal from Capitol Steps," *CS*, October 27, 1964.

19. Mrs. Marvin to Harriet, undated note, "SC State House Grounds" folder, box 35, REM Landscape Architectural Collection, SoCar.

20. "State House Speech," "State Capital Grounds Update 880810" folder, box 75, REM Landscape Architectural Collection, SoCar.

21. REM to Furman E. McEachern Jr., February 14, 1967, "SC State House Grounds" folder, box 35, REM Landscape Architectural Collection, SoCar.

22. REM quoted in J. William Thompson, "Southern Savior," *Landscape Architecture Magazine* 87, no. 6 (June 1997): 77. See also Sarah Georgia Harrison Hall, "Robert E. Marvin: Southern Agrarian Meets Modernist," *Landscape Journal* 36, no. 2 (2017): 53–71; and Sarah Georgia Harrison, "Modernist Redesign in a Traditional Southern Context: The Robert Marvin Residence in Walterboro, South Carolina," in *Exploring the Boundaries of Historic Landscape Preservation* (Clemson, SC: Clemson University Digital Press, 2008), 180–91.

23. "State House Speech."

24. REM to Furman McEachern Jr., August 16, 1967, "SC State House Grounds" folder, box 35, REM Landscape Architectural Collection, SoCar.

25. REM to Bill Carlisle, Memorandum, January 8, 1969 and "Methods for Landscape Construction," undated, both "Governor Byrns' [*sic*] Statue Location" folder, box 8, REM Landscape Architectural Collection, SoCar.

26. Robert E. Marvin to Bill Lyles, Memorandum, December 9, 1968, "Governor Byrns' [*sic*] Statue Location" folder, box 8, REM Landscape Architectural Collection, SoCar.

27. Levona Page, "Grounds at State House to Be Picturesque Mall," *CS*, November 26, 1972.

Capitol Complex Master Plan

28. Page, "Boom Puts SC in Space Race."
29. "The State House," *CS*, June 13, 1967.
30. Levona Page, "Even Government Has Growing Pains," *CS*, April 21, 1968.
31. W. G. Lyles to Robert E. McNair, July 8, 1968, box 82, Robert E. McNair Papers, Modern Political Collections, UofSC.
32. "Bulldozers Begin Work on Capitol Complex," *CS*, August 3, 1969.
33. Philip G. Grose Jr., "Bond Cut Try Fails; Filibuster Follows," *CS*, May 31, 1968; Peggy Whitaker, "Bristow, Powell Debate," *CR*, September 25, 1968.
34. "State House Speech."
35. See Stephanie Gray, "Cornell Arms," National Register of Historic Places Nomination Form, listed 2019.
36. *Report of the State Budget and Control Board, Division of General Services, to the General Assembly of South Carolina, for the Period Ending June 30, 1966*, 27, SoCar.
37. "The State House," *CS*, May 18, 1965.
38. John A. Montgomery, "Columbia's Defense Against Chaos," *CR*, July 16, 1971; "Plan Allows Easy Access Downtown," *CS*, July 5, 1970; "Capital City Recipe: Mix Well and Simmer," *CS*, April 5, 1970.
39. Doxiadis Associates, Inc., WS&A, and LBC&W, "Central City Columbia SC Master Plan" (n.p., December 1969); Doxiadis Associates, Inc., WS&A, and LBC&W, "Central City, Columbia, S.C. . . . Year 2000," SoCar.
40. "Parking Facility Bids to Be Opened Thursday," *CS*, April 18, 1965.
41. John A. Montgomery, *History of Wilbur Smith and Associates, 1952–1984* (Columbia: Wilbur Smith and Associates, 1985).

Furman McEachern Jr. Parking Garage

42. W. D. Workman, "Plain Talk," *CS*, February 20, 1963.
43. John A. Jackle and Keith A. Sculle, *Lots of Parking: Land Use in a Car Culture* (Charlottesville: University of Virginia Press, 2004), 151–52.
44. "Put Them Underground," *CS*, February 2, 1967; "Proposed Capital Complex," *CR*, April 17, 1968.
45. Wilbur Smith & Associates, *Parking Program, South Carolina State*

Capitol Building Complex, Columbia, South Carolina (prepared for the State of South Carolina, 1967), 65.

46. "Parking Garage Permit Issued," *CS*, August 27, 1970; "Capital Complex Parking Available," *CS*, October 11, 1971.

47. "Capital Complex Parking Available."

48. "State House Escalator Finished," *CS*, January 31, 1978.

49. John O'Connor, "Capitol Security to Be Upgraded," *CS*, October 4, 2007.

50. "The Live Wire," *CR*, May 15, 1973; Al Lanier, "State House Building Goes on and On," *CR*, January 18, 1973.

51. Clark Surratt, "A Dedication: Former Gov. McNair a Permanent Part of State's Capitol Complex," *CS*, October 31, 1981.

52. Fred Monk, "Capitol Complex to Be Bicentennial Project," *CR*, August 10, 1974; "State Parking Facility Named for Furman E. McEachern Jr.," *CR*, June 18, 1979.

53. "McEachern Eulogized during Ceremonies," *CR*, April 24, 1980. Walter B. Brown, Director of Sinking Funds and Property, very briefly served as an interim director between the agency's founding in July 1964 and McEachern's appointment.

Edgar A. Brown Building and the Solomon Blatt Building

54. Robert G. Liming, "Texas Firm to Build Office Building," *CS*, July 9, 1971.

55. "New State Building Welcome," *CR*, July 21, 1971.

56. Fran Zupan, "Tribute in Concrete Honors Sen. Brown," *CR*, June 12, 1975; "Former Senator Brown Dies of Crash Injuries," *CS*, June 25, 1975.

57. W. D. Workman Jr., "'The Bishop from Barnwell' Was a Scrapper to the End," *CS*, June 25, 1975; "Wade Hampton Office Building Dedicated; Gridley Is Speaker," *CS*, May 15, 1940.

L. Marion Gressette Building

58. "Crowded Skyline," *CS*, October 1, 1972; Robert M. Hitt III, "New Offices Cost State $20.3 Million," *CR*, July 11, 1978; Willian S. Tracener, "Construction of Capitol Complex Defended," *CS*, January 25, 1979; "Preside at Ground Breaking," *CS*, June 4, 1975.

59. Levona Page, "Legislators Will Soon Have Their Own Private Offices," *CS*, September 20, 1976.

60. "25 House Members Think Office Space in Complex a Waste," *CS*, April 6, 1978.

61. Marilyn Thompson, "Building Hailed as 'Durable' Symbol," *CS*, February 21, 1979.

62. Thompson, "Building Hailed"; Grose, "Bond Cut Try Fails; Filibuster Follows."

Rembert C. Dennis Building

63. "New Highway Building to Rise Here," *CS*, August 6, 1950.

64. R. E. Grier, "Around the State House," *CS*, March 5, 1951; "More Efficiency Is Found in Big Highway Building," *CR*, February 25, 1953. The South Carolina Supreme Court ruled in favor of the state's right to operate a restaurant in the building after local restaurant owners argued that it had an unfair advantage. See "Highway Building Restaurant Case in Top Court," *CS*, January 23, 1953; and "Beck to Run Restaurant in Highway Department," *CR*, January 22, 1954.

65. Kenneth M. Hare, "Capitol Expansion May Pave Way for Highway Department Relocation," *CS*, May 20, 1973; W. Clark Surratt, "SCHD Accepts Headquarters," *CS*, February 22, 1974.

66. "Retrofit or Rape," *CR*, January 29, 1979.

67. Douglas Mauldin, "Renovation May Cost as Much as Constructing New Building," *CS*, May 24, 1977; "Renovation May Be More than Legislators Wanted," *CR*, January 24, 1979.

68. "Sen. Dennis Honored at Building Dedication," *CS*, July 15, 1981.

69. See Joan Mower, "Officials Looking for Sculptor to Cast Bronze Bust of Dennis," *CR*, January 29, 1980; and Hitt, "New Offices Cost State $20.3 Million." On McWhorter, see obituary, *CS*, February 20, 2011.

Richardson Square Marker

70. Levona Page, "1972 Legislative Action," *CS*, June 30, 1972.

71. "Generals and Groceries Aid in Naming Streets of Columbia," *CR*, June 2, 1934; Robert P. Broadwater, *American Generals of the Revolutionary War* (Jefferson, NC: McFarland, 2007), 119.

72. Samuel P. Manning of Spartanburg proposed the measure. Robert G. Liming, "USC Bond Ceiling Hike Requested," *CS*, June 7, 1972.

73. Advertisements often specified locations of businesses as "Richardson (Main) Street." See "Commissioner's Sale," *Columbia Daily Phoenix*, December 29, 1865. Few ads featured "Richardson" at all by 1899, with some specifying "Main, formerly Richardson, street." See "Master's Sale," *CS*, November 18, 1899.

74. "Marker to Honor Statesman," *CS*, July 1, 1976.

Capitol Complex Marker

75. Jack Bass, "Robert McNair, Governor of South Carolina in the '60s, Dies at 83," *New York Times*, November 24, 2007.
76. Surratt, "A Dedication."
77. "Renovation May Be More than Legislators Wanted."

Columbia Bicentennial Time Capsule

78. "Capital Report," *CS*, December 15, 1986.
79. Columbia Bicentennial Committee, *Columbia's Bicentennial Celebration* (1986), RCPL; "Bicentennial Is Apt Focus on What City Is," *CS*, January 1, 1986.
80. Michael Lewis, "The Wait Begins," *CS*, January 1, 1987.

Strom Thurmond Monument

81. Thurmond's forty-eight-year Senate career was topped by Robert Byrd's fifty-one years representing West Virginia and Daniel Inouye forty-nine years representing Hawaii.
82. See Joseph Crespino, *Strom Thurmond's America* (New York: Hill & Wang, 2012).
83. "Governor Signs Bill for Thurmond Statue," *CS*, April 1, 1997.
84. Cindi Ross Scoppe, "Courson's Year Looks at Carolina History," *CS*, July 10, 1997.
85. Jeffrey Day, "Strom Designers Face a Statue of Limitations," *CS*, October 9, 1997; Sid Gaulden, "Artist Behrends Chosen to Design Thurmond," *CS*, January 14, 1998.
86. Davis, "Funding South Carolina's Monuments," 32–33. Corporate donations were capped at $75,000.
87. Jesse J. Holland, "Plans for Black Statue Slow but Thurmond Model On," *CS*, October 12, 1997.
88. Michelle R. Davis, "Thurmond Statue to Be Unveiled Today," *CS*, December 4, 1999.
89. Lee Bandy, "1,200 Cheer as South Carolina Unveils New Monument," *CS*, December 5, 1999.
90. "Honoring the Senator's Daughter," *Charleston Post and Courier*, January 15, 2004. Thurmond was twenty-two years old when Washington-Williams was born, and the two met for the first time when she was sixteen.

91. Clay Barbour, "Bill Would Add Name to Thurmond Monument," *Charleston Post and Courier*, January 14, 2004; Joseph Crespino, "The Scarred Stone: The Strom Thurmond Monument," *Southern Spaces*, April 29, 2010, https://southernspaces.org/2010/scarred-stone-strom-thurmond-monument/.

92. Jennifer Talhelm, "Thurmond Family History Now Set in Stone," CS, July 2, 2004.

African American History Monument

93. Michael Sponhour, "Written in Stone: Can Panel Sketch SC Black History onto a Single State House Monument," *CS*, August 18, 1996.

94. Prince, *Rally 'Round the Flag, Boys!*, 106–7; Dell Upton, *What Can and Can't Be Said: Race, Uplift, and Monument Building in the Contemporary South* (New Haven: Yale University Press, 2015), 176–84.

95. Lee Bandy, "Black-History Monument 'Off and Running,'" CS, December 15, 1998; Sponhour, "Written in Stone." The failed 1994 legislation was called the Heritage Act.

96. Prince, *Rally 'Round the Flag, Boys!*, 195–247.

97. Upton, *What Can and Can't Be Said*, 178–84.

98. Kenneth A. Harris, "Minor, Not Monumental, Delays on African-American Marker," CS, December 3, 2000.

99. Upton, *What Can and Can't Be Said*, 178–81. Since completing South Carolina's sculpture, Dwight sculpted the African American History Memorial for the Texas State House grounds in Austin (unveiled 2016).

100. House Concurrent Resolution Bill 4119, 2001–2002, South Carolina State Legislature; Upton, *What Can and Can't Be Said*, 184.

101. To protect the image, a railing was added around the image of the ship shortly after it was unveiled. See Upton, *What Can and Can't Be Said*, 187.

102. Upton, *What Can and Can't Be Said*, 181–84.

103. Senator Darrell Jackson quoted in Sponhour, "Written in Stone."

104. Chuck Crumbo, "Marker to Tell Black History; Groundbreaking for African-American Monument to Take Place This Morning," CS, May 11, 2000.

105. Valerie Bauerlein, "Granite, Bronze and Triumph," CS, March 25, 2001.

106. Upton, *What Can and Can't Be Said*, 193–95.

107. Nikki Finney, poem read 2001, revised 2021. Email to author, February

5, 2021. Thank you to Professor Finney for providing permission to publish this poem.

108. Bauerlein, "Granite, Bronze and Triumph"; Davis, "Funding South Carolina's Monuments," 34. BMW opened its largest manufacturing plant outside of Germany in Spartanburg, South Carolina, in 1994.

South Carolina Law Enforcement Memorial and Armed Forces Monument

109. Christina Lee Knauss, "Fallen Officers Honored," *CS*, February 16, 2006.

110. "Final Remembrances," *CS*, August 11, 2005.

111. Rick Brundrett, "Number of SC Officers Killed on Duty in 2002 Ties Record," *CS*, May 8, 2003.

112. House Concurrent Resolution 4119, May 15, 2001, South Carolina State Legislature.

113. Young had long worked for the Georgia Marble Company designing sculptures for cemeteries and other memorials. See *Elberton Graniteer* 33, no. 2 (Summer 1989).

114. "Senate Likely to Extend Session," *CS*, June 2, 2003; Lee Bandy, "Sanford 'has got gall,'" *CS*, February 26, 2006.

115. Bandy, "Sanford 'has got gall.'"

116. Knauss, "Fallen Officers Honored."

117. Bandy, "Sanford 'has got gall.'"

118. Loren Thomas, "Fallen South Carolina Officers Remembered during Memorial Service," WLTX, November 9, 2018, https://www.wltx.com/article/news/fallen-officers-honored-at-law-enforcement-memorial-service/101-1c0a52a8-d1c1-4cd7-9ff0-f56fee5f7ecb.

119. Kenneth A. Harris, "Monument to Honor All SC Veterans," *CS*, December 25, 2002.

120. Joseph S. Stroud and Kenneth A. Harris, "Flag Grouping to Be Proposed: Two Richland Senators Hope to Alter Compromise with a 'Military Commons' of Flags," *CS*, May 16, 2000.

121. Stroud and Harris, "Flag Grouping to Be Proposed."

122. Harris, "Monument to Honor All SC Veterans." The World War II Monument was started in September 2001 and dedicated in April 2004.

123. Chuck Crumbo, "New Monument Tops Off Veterans' Big Day in SC," *CS*, November 12, 2005.

124. Dawn Hinshaw, "Crowding In," *CS*, July 24, 2003; Dawn Hinshaw, "Final Remembrances," *CS*, August 11, 2005.

125. A77, R138, H3699, General Bill, passed June 5, 2007, signed by governor June 13, 2007; Roddie A. Burris, "Panel Calls for Longer Moratorium," *CS*, January 26, 2007; Cindi Ross Scoppe, "Don't Count on New Statue to Honor Black Warriors," *CS*, December 5, 2017.

Index

Page numbers in italics refer to photographs and images.

abolitionism, 28

African American History Monument, 119, *120*, 120–24, *123*, 125, 126

Allston, Robert Francis Withers, 143n55

American Revolution, 17–19, 113. *See also* Partisan Generals Monument; Washington statue

antilynching legislation, 85, 87

Armed Forces Monument, 125, 127–28, *128*

Art Deco design, 77–78

Assembly Street, 96, 98, 127–28. *See also* Columbia, master plans

Bacon, Rebecca, 51–52

Baker, Mary Craig, 19

Beaux-Arts design, 16, 40, 97, 101

Behrends, William, 119

Bissett, Thomas J., 102

Blacks United for Action rally, 5

Blatt Building, *92*, 101, 102, 104, 105, 106–8, 109, 112

Blatt, Solomon, 108

bronze casting, 21

Brown Building, *92*, 101, 104, 105, 106–8, 109

Brown, Edgar Allan, *107*, 108; bronze bust of, 112

Brown, Henry Kirke, 12–13, 20, 24–28

Brutalist architecture, 41–42, 91, 100, 107–8, 109, 110

Butler, Andrew Pickens, 143n55

Butler, Pierce Mason, 30–31

Byrnes, James "Jimmy" F., 82, 84, 93–96

Byrnes, Maude, 96

Byrnes Monument, *93*, 93–96, *95*, 118

Calhoun Building, 17, 35, 41–42, 76, 78, 100–101, 105, 108–9; photographs of, *74*, *75*, *105*, *111*

Calhoun, John C., 7, 10–11, 12; plaster cast of, location, 144n60, 149n25

Calhoun statue, 42

Canova, Antonio, 20

Capitol Complex, 17, 77–78, *92*, 96, 99–115, *101*

Capitol Complex marker, *114*, 114–15

Carlisle, William A., 102

Churubusco, battle of, 30

Cincinnatus, 20

City Beautiful movement, 40, 49

Civic Improvement League, 40, 42

Civil Rights Act (1957), 118

Civil Rights Movement, 85

Civil War, 7, 13, 22–23, 28; centennial, 88

Classical Revival architecture, 9, 11–12, 110

Cobb-Hunter, Gilda, 119, 121

Cold War and communism, 71, 72, 86–87

Columbia, burning of, 7, 13–14, 22–24
Columbia bicentennial time capsule, 115–16, *116*
Columbia Committee of the National Society of the Colonial Dames of America, 113–14
Columbia, master plans: by Kelsey & Guild, 40–41, *41*; by LBC&W, WA&A, and Doxiadis, 99–104
Columbia Stone Company, 81
Confederate battle flag, 87–89, *88–89*, 118–19, 121, 127
Confederate Monument, 33, 39, 43–46, 87–88, 96, 127; photographs of, *44, 45, 88–89, 91*
Confederate Women's Monument, 42, 50, 54–57, *55, 57*, 99, 161n9
Consolidated Granite Company, *66*
convict-lease labor, 15, 22, 39
Courson, John, 118–19, 127–29
Craft, John Richard, 161n6
Crown, Cork & Seal Company, 73
cultural landscape, definition of, 3
Cunningham, Ann Pamela, 73

Daughters of the American Revolution, 51–53, 72–73. *See also* Partisan Generals Monument
David Dubose Gaillard Camp (camp of South Carolina Spanish War Veterans), 62–63
Davis Granite Company, 53
Davis, Jefferson, 22, 67–68, 69
Davis Memorial Highway Marker, 67, *68*, 68–69, 96
Dennis Building, 100–101, 102, 105, 108–9, 110–12, *111*, 115
Dennis, Rembert Coney, 112; relief sculpture of, 112
disenfranchisement and enfranchisement, 5, 8, 84–85

Dixiecrats, 118
Doxiadis, Constantinos, 103–4
Duncan, Walter E., 80
Dwight, Ed, 122–23

eagles, 26, 31, 32, 125
enslaved people, 64–65, 67; depiction of, 26–28, *27*; labor for grounds and construction, 13, 31, 121. *See also* African American History Monument
Evans, Matilda, 123

fasces, 20, 26
Felder, James, 90
Fielding, Herbert, 90
Finney, Ernst, Jr., 123
Finney, Nikky, 123–24
Floyd, George: protests for, 2
fountain, proposed, 97, *97*
Frazier, Joe, 123
funding, 109–10, 112, 125–27, *128*; Capitol Complex, 102; private, 31, 44–46, 47–48, 51–53, 94, 119, 121, 124, 159n179

Gervais Street, 98, 155n125; widening of, 69, 96. *See also* Columbia, master plans
Gibson, Althea, 123
Gillespie, Dizzy, 123
Gist, William Henry, 26
Glenn, Alvin S., 127
Gorham Manufacturing Company, 63
Granby Quarry, 13
Great Seal of the United States, 26, 145n71
Great Society, 90
Greene, Nathanael, 17
Gressette Building, *92*, 101, *105*, 108–10, *109*, 112

Gressette, Lawrence Marion, 110; bronze bust of, 112

Haley, Nikki, 89
Hammarskold, Peter Hjalmar, 11
Hampton Building, 17, 35, 41–42, 51, 77, 77–78, 100–101, 105, 108–9, *111*
Hampton Monument, *xvi*, 1, 19, 42, 46–51, *47, 48, 50,* 54, 78, 82, 99
Hampton, Wade, 37–38, 46, 47, 79, 82–84, 122; tomb of, *54*
Hayne, Robert Young, 25–26
Heritage Act (2000), 88–89
Hibbard, Frederick C., 84
Highway Building, 41–42, 101, *111*. *See also* Dennis Building
Hiker. See Spanish War Veterans Monument
Hoban, James, 82, 139n2
Hope, depiction of, 26, *27*
Hopkins and Baker, 78
Hopkins, Baker & Gill, 110–12
Houdon, Jean-Antoine, 19–20, *21,* 145n72
Hubard, James William, 20–22
hurricanes, 33

Independence Saving Bonds, 86–87
International Style architecture, 41, 110

Jackson, Darrell, 119, 127
Jackson, Jesse, 123
Jefferson, Thomas, 20
Jim Crow, 5, 84–85
Johnson, I. S. Leevy, 90
Johnson, Lyndon B., 90, 96
Jones, Elaine, 127
Justice, depiction of, 26

Kelsey & Guild, 40–41
Kelsey, Harlan P., 40–41, 96

King, Rodney, 126
Kitson, Theo Alice Ruggles, 63–64
Korean War, 87
Ku Klux Klan, 8

Lafaye, Lafaye, and Fair, 78
Lafaye and Lafaye, 66
Lamar, Dorothy, 71
Law Enforcement Memorial, 122, 125–27, *126,* 128
Lee, Harry, 17
Lee Memorial Highway Marker, 67, 69–71, *70,* 73
Lee Memorial trees, *72, 73*
Lee, Robert E., 67–68, *69*
Liberty Bell replica, 86, *86, 91,* 99
Liberty, depiction of, 26
Lincoln Highway, 68
Loftis, Michael, 125
Lost Cause, 39, 42, 46–47, 69
Lunsford grave, 17–19, *18,* 37
Lunsford, Swanson, 17–18
Lyles, Bissett, Carlisle & Wolff (LBC&W), 90, 97–112
Lyles, William G., 101–2

Main Street (Richardson Street), 11, 46, 49, 72, 113. *See also* Columbia, master plans
Manning, John Lawrence, 11
Marion, Francis, 51
Marvin, Robert, 37, 66, 94, 96–99
Maybank, Burnet Rhett, 63
McConnell, Glenn, 121
McDuffie, George, 25–26
McEachern, Furman, Jr., 106
McEachern Parking Garage, 91, *92,* 99, 101–2, 104–6, *105*
McNair, Gordon, Johnson & Karasiewicz, 102, 112
McNair, Robert, 97, 100, 106, 114–15
McNair, Ronald, 123

McWhorter, Jean, 112, 115
Medary, Milton, Jr., 76
Memorial Trees, 71–73
Mexican-American War, 30
Milburn, Frank Pierce, 15–16
Milliken, Roger, 94
Monument Avenue (Richmond, Va.), 39, 49
Monument to the Confederate Dead. *See* Confederate Monument
Monument to the Women of the Confederacy. *See* Confederate Women's Monument
moratorium on future monuments, 125, 129
Mother Emanuel AME Church, 89
Muldoon, Walton & Company, 45

NAACP, 85, 88
National Sculpture Society, 63
Neilson, J. Crawford, 14–15
Nicoli, Carlo, 46
Niernsee, Frank McHenry, 15
Niernsee, John Rudolph, 11, 12, 14, 24, 81
Nixon, Richard, 96
nullification, 25

Orange, Jimmy, 1
Orangeburg Massacre, 115

Palmetto Monument, 29, 29–33, 32, 37, 39, 82, 91, 99
Palmetto Regiment, 30–31
parking, 43, 91, 96, 97, 100. *See also* McEachern Parking Garage
Parks, Charles Cropper, 94–95
Partisan Generals Monument, 19, 42, 50, 51–54, 52
pedestrian paths, 37–39, 41, 82, 98–105, 108–10, 117; in photographs

and images, 50, 85, 91, 98, 101, 133–36
Phillips, Nancy, 59
Pickens, Andrew, 51
Pierce, Franklin, 12
police brutality, 2
ponds, 37–39
Public Works Administration, 77–78, 158n159

Quinn, Edward Thomas, 66

Reconstruction, 7, 84, 122; legislature of, 14, 23–24. *See also* "redemption"
"redemption," 34, 37, 39, 42, 44, 46–47, 49–50
Renaissance Revival architecture, 74
Revolutionary War, Civil War, and redemption, continuity of, 53–54
Richards, John Gardiner, Jr., 84
Richardson, Richard, 113
Richardson, Sara, 51–52
Richardson Square marker, 113, 113–14
Richardson Street. *See* Main Street (Richardson Street)
Robertson, Annie, 51–53
Roosevelt, Franklin D., 94
Ruckstull, Frederick Wellington, 42, 49–50, 51–57, 79, 144n60
Russell, Robert, 36–37
Rutledge Building, 103

Salley, Alexander Samuel, Jr., 24, 50–51, 79–82, 142nn35–36
Sanders Middle School, 124
Sanford, Mark, 127
Schwagerl, Edward Otto, 37, 98
Scott, Tommy, 59

Seabrook, Whitemarsh Benjamin, 10–11

secession, 13, 26

segregation and desegregation, 78, 87–88, 94, 110, 115, 118

Senate Street, 11, 35, 56–57, 74, 97–99

September 11, 2001, 128

Shand, Gadsden E., 141n29

Sherman, William Tecumseh, 78–79

Simkins, Modjeska, 85

Simmons, Hubert D., 107

Sims, James Marion, 64–65, 67

Sims Monument, 64–67, 65, 66, 84, 99

Sims statue (New York City), 64–65, 67

slavery and sectional crisis, 20–23; and proslavery advocates, 25, 28. *See also* Civil War

Smith, James, 104

Smith, Wilbur, 104

Snowden, Yates, 54

Sons of the American Revolution, 19

South Carolina Confederate Relic Room and Military Museum, 89

South Carolina Congress of Parents and Teachers, 73

South Carolina Department of Parks, Recreation and Tourism, 107, 115

South Carolina Division of General Services, 100, 106

South Carolina Fraternal Order of Police, 125

South Carolina Medical Association, 65

South Carolina Medical Association Auxiliary, 64–66

South Carolina Monument Association (SCMA), 44–46

South Carolina Monument to the Confederate Dead. *See* Confederate Monument

South Carolina Spanish War Veterans camp, 62–63

South Carolina State Court of Appeals, 76

South Carolina Supreme Court, 76, 165n64

Spanish-American War, 58–64

Spanish-American War cannon, 59, 59–60, 60, 99

Spanish-American War monuments, 58–64

Spanish War Veterans Monument, 62, 62–64, 83

spatial relationships between monuments, xiv–xv, 39, 46, 51, 53–54, 99, 133–36

State House, first in Columbia, 10, 13, 36–37, 79; as inadequate, 7; marker, 81, 81–82

State House, second in Columbia: burning and destruction during Civil War, 7, 13, 13–14, 28, 32; completion, 16, 16–17; designs for, 11–13, 12, 108; dome, 15, 16, 16–17, 40; funding for, 14–15; interior of, 15, 17; labor of Black convicts, 15; and monuments, photographs of, 15, 91; pediment, 27; porticos, 14–15, 15; roof of, 14, 14; sculpture on North Facade, 24–28, 25; stars, 79–81, 80

State House grounds: burning of, 78–82; expansion of, 1, 35, 41; funding for, 34, 43; improvement of, 42–43, 96–99; master plans, 37, 38, 40–41, 41, 96–99; neglect of, 19, 40; use of, 90–92, 97–99, 98

state sovereignty over federal power, narrative of, 20–24, 26, 39, 47–51, 79, 118
States' Rights Democratic Party, 118
Sterner, Harold, 66
Stripped Classical architecture, 77–78
Stuckey, Daisy Lee, 65
Sumter, Thomas, 51

Tatum, Harold, 76
Thurmond, James Strom, 117–19
Thurmond Monument, 117, 117–19, 118, 128
Tillman, Benjamin Ryan, 82–84, 94
Tillman Monument, 63, 82–85, 83, 85, 94
time capsules, 96, 115–17, 116
tornadoes, 33
Trescot, William Henry, 45
Trinity Cathedral, xiv, 31, 49, 50, 54, 94, 99, 131
Truman, Harry, 87, 94, 118

Union National Bank Building, 75
United Confederate Veterans (UCV), 55–57
United Daughters of the Confederacy (UDC), 48, 54, 55–57, 67–71, 73

US Capitol, 25, 28
USS Maine, 58
USS Maine gun, 61–62

vandalism, 50–51, 66
Vesey, Denmark, 123

Walker, George Edward, 11
War Memorial Building, 79, 158n159
Washington memorial trees, 71–73
Washington statue, 19–24, 23, 39, 46, 50; cane of, 23–24, 79
Washington statue at Virginia State Capitol, 21
Washington-Williams, Essie Mae, 118, 119
Werner, Christopher, 29–30, 31–32, 33
White, Edward Brickell, 30–31
Wilbur Smith & Associates (WS&A), 97, 99, 100–101, 103–5
Wilson, Charles C., 17
Wolff, Louis M., 102
Works Progress Administration, 33
World War I, 158n159
World War II, 60, 94

yellow fever, 18
Young, Robert P., 126